Digital Curation Projects Made Easy

LIBRARY INFORMATION TECHNOLOGY ASSOCIATION (LITA) GUIDES

Marta Mestrovic Deyrup, Ph.D.
Acquisitions Editor, Library Information and Technology Association, a division of the American Library Association
The Library Information Technology Association (LITA) Guides provide information and guidance on topics related to cutting edge technology for library and IT specialists.

Written by top professionals in the field of technology, the guides are sought after by librarians wishing to learn a new skill or to become current in today's best practices.

Each book in the series has been overseen editorially since conception by LITA and reviewed by LITA members with special expertise in the specialty area of the book.

Established in 1966, LITA is the division of the American Library Association (ALA) that provides its members and the library and information science community as a whole with a forum for discussion, an environment for learning, and a program for actions on the design, development, and implementation of automated and technological systems in the library and information science field.

Approximately 25 LITA Guides were published by Neal-Schuman and ALA between 2007 and 2015. Rowman & Littlefield took over publication of the series beginning in late 2015. Books in the series published by Rowman & Littlefield are:

Digitizing Flat Media: Principles and Practices
The Librarian's Introduction to Programming Languages
Library Service Design: A LITA Guide to Holistic Assessment, Insight, and Improvement
Data Visualization: A Guide to Visual Storytelling for Librarians
Mobile Technologies in Libraries: A LITA Guide
Innovative LibGuides Applications
Integrating LibGuides into Library Websites
Protecting Patron Privacy: A LITA Guide
The LITA Leadership Guide: The Librarian as Entrepreneur, Leader, and Technologist
Using Social Media to Build Library Communities: A LITA Guide
Managing Library Technology: A LITA Guide
The LITA Guide to No- or Low-Cost Technology Tools for Libraries
Big Data Shocks: An Introduction to Big Data for Librarians and Information Professionals
The Savvy Academic Librarian's Guide to Technological Innovation: Moving Beyond the Wow Factor
Augmented and Virtual Reality in Libraries
Digital Curation Projects Made Easy: A Step-By-Step Guide for Libraries, Archives, and Museums

Digital Curation Projects Made Easy

A Step-by-Step Guide for Libraries, Archives, and Museums

Carmen Cowick

ROWMAN & LITTLEFIELD
Lanham • Boulder • New York • London

Published by Rowman & Littlefield
An imprint of The Rowman & Littlefield Publishing Group, Inc.
4501 Forbes Boulevard, Suite 200, Lanham, Maryland 20706
www.rowman.com

Unit A, Whitacre Mews, 26-34 Stannary Street, London SE11 4AB

Copyright © 2018 by American Library Association

All rights reserved. No part of this book may be reproduced in any form or by any electronic or mechanical means, including information storage and retrieval systems, without written permission from the publisher, except by a reviewer who may quote passages in a review.

British Library Cataloguing in Publication Information Available

Library of Congress Cataloging-in-Publication Data Available

ISBN 9781538103500 (cloth: alk. paper) | ISBN 9781538103517 (pbk. : alk. paper) | ISBN 9781538103524 (electronic)

∞ ™ The paper used in this publication meets the minimum requirements of American National Standard for Information Sciences Permanence of Paper for Printed Library Materials, ANSI/NISO Z39.48-1992.

Printed in the United States of America

Contents

Preface	vii
Part I: The Basics	**1**
1 Introduction	3
2 What Every Project Needs to Get Started	11
Part II: Digital Curation Projects Step-By-Step	**29**
3 General Guidelines	31
4 Photograph Collections	47
5 Newspaper Collections	61
6 Rare Books	75
7 Art Collections	89
8 Oral Histories	99
Bibliography	115
Index	119
About the Author	125

Preface

Taking on a digital curation project may feel like a daunting task. It seems like every day there is news about a new digital project that some organization is undertaking, and it is not hard to feel left in the dust. Rest assured that you are not alone; many organizations would very much like to take on a digital curation project but simply do not know where to begin. While there are a variety of resources out there, very few focus on the absolute, complete beginner. *Digital Curation Projects Made Easy* is aimed at the digital curation novice and is broken down into two sections for an easy grasp on the subject.

The first part of this book will start with a basic introduction to the topic, focusing on defining digitization, digital preservation, digital curation, and their importance; if digitization is right for your project; and what is needed to get a digital project started. The first chapter contains general guidelines that will be applicable to any and every digital curation project you choose. Each following chapter will look at a variety of projects that are most popular with libraries, archives, and museums and will have specific guidelines that are unique to its corresponding project.

Digital Curation Projects Made Easy is not intended to be read from front to back; think of this book as more of a reference guide, something to keep on the shelf and pull out each time you take on a new digital curation project. Each chapter in part II of this book is self-sufficient for the most part, containing step-by-step guides for each project, with examples, templates, and checklists to help you through.

Part I

The Basics

Chapter One

Introduction

Before you can begin to take on a digital curation project, we must discuss the differences between digitization, digital preservation, and digital curation. A digital curation project will involve both digitization and digital preservation, but they are not the same. Let's examine these terms in depth.

DEFINING DIGITIZATION

Digitization is the process of taking a physical or analog object and creating a digital copy of that object. Digitization is often mistaken for digital preservation, and many times they are used interchangeably even though they are not the same thing. It is important to understand that digitization is not preservation; digitization is about providing access, while digital preservation is about caring for the digital object in the same way you would care for a physical or analog object. In fact, your digital object will probably need much more care than any physical object in your collection because of issues like bit rot, file format obsolescence, and hardware/application obsolescence. In other words, scanning or photographing an object to create a digital object is digitization, while digital preservation involves a different set of goals and tasks, which we will discuss later on in this chapter.

THE ADVANTAGES OF DIGITIZATION

Digitizing items can be costly in terms of both time and money, so it is important to be aware of the many advantages of digitizing items in your collection. These advantages can help convince administrators, board members, and other interested parties that digitizing your objects is worthwhile. Let's take a look at the most common advantages in detail.

Expanded Access

Unlike the physical items in your collection, digital objects offer access to those who cannot come to your facilities. This means users from another city, state, or country can view your materials. Expanded access increases your organization's visibility, opening the door to future collaboration with other organizations and providing opportunities for future funding as well. It is not only physical barriers that are removed with digital preservation but also time barriers. Your digital items are available to users any time of the day and any time of the year. You will see an increase in users when they know they can research items in the middle of the night or on a holiday.

Aids in the Preservation of Analog or Physical Items

If your digital objects are reformatted from physical objects, then your researchers will most likely no longer have to request to view the originals. This means that preservation of analog or physical items can be reduced, because wear and tear on these objects has been minimized. Some rare objects can be quite costly to preserve, so it may be wise to consider digitally preserving these items.

Aids in the Event of a Disaster

If a disaster should destroy your physical collection, you will still have access to it if you had it digitized. When Hurricane Sandy struck in 2012, the floodwaters wiped out most of the Ehrman Medical Library's on-site print collections at New York University's Langone Medical Center, and while the storm also knocked out essential equipment and access to digital resources and services, eventually those were up and running again. The same could not be said of their on-site print collection.[1]

You may also want to consider digitization for the following reasons:

- You are experiencing a shortage of physical storage space. When you digitize these objects you will no longer need immediate access to the originals, so it is possible to store these items in off-site storage and free up your on-site physical storage space.
- Your objects are fragile. Perhaps your collection consists of very brittle rare books or degrading film or photographs. The digitization of these delicate objects will allow users to maintain access to them.
- An example of this can be found at the Rochester Public Library. They own a rather large and important collection of regional history materi-

al that dates back to the early nineteenth century. These materials serve as an important resource for students, educators, historians, and genealogists, but much of the heavily utilized collection is in such fragile condition that portions are in danger of being damaged beyond recovery, so they have decided to digitize these items.[2]
- You want to raise the profile of your organization. Digitizing your collections demonstrates your organization's commitment to education, public access, and scholarship, and would help with obtaining funding and other necessary resources for digital preservation.
- You want to collaborate with another organization. If there is another organization that has a collection that is complementary to yours, you may consider digitizing your items and creating a collaborative project with the other organization. In addition, many funding opportunities require collaboration, and partnerships between your organization and others can be an excellent opportunity to cultivate strategic connections. An example of this is the California State University Japanese-American Digitization Project. This project united collections from at least thirteen campuses in the California State University system to create a picture of what the lives of Japanese-Americans were like during World War II.[3]
- You have the funds to digitize and preserve the objects in this collection. Take into consideration the cost of getting your project off the ground and maintaining this new digital collection. You will have to invest in new technology every few years, and the staff will have to learn the latest systems and applications.

DEFINING DIGITAL PRESERVATION

The Preservation and Reformatting Section of the Association for Library Collections & Technical Services, which is a division of the American Library Association, has three definitions for digital preservation; a short, medium, and long definition. Let's take a look at these in detail.

The short definition says that "digital preservation combines policies, strategies and actions that ensure access to digital content over time."[4] This definition provides a very basic idea of what digital preservation is without going into too much detail; it lets us know that there are various procedures, approaches, and tactics that you must use in order to make sure that your digital items are accessible for users not only today, but in the future as well.

The medium definition states that "digital preservation combines policies, strategies and actions to ensure access to reformatted and born digital content regardless of the challenges of media failure and technological change. The goal of digital preservation is the accurate rendering of authenticated content over time."⁵ This definition mentions that you are preserving both reformatted and born digital content. Your digital collection will most likely consist of a combination of these two types of objects. Reformatted digital objects are digital items that were originally in analog or physical form and then reconfigured into a digital format. Born digital objects mean just that: they were born digital; they were originally created in a digital format. This definition also provides us with a more defined goal: to create an accurate rendering of authenticated content over time. In other words, one of our goals is to make sure our digital objects are authentic. We can define authenticity as "the trustworthiness of a record as a record; i.e., the quality of a record that is what it purports to be and that is free from tampering or corruption."⁶

Now we come to the long definition of digital preservation, which states, "Digital preservation policies document an organization's commitment to preserve digital content for future use; specify file formats to be preserved and the level of preservation to be provided; and ensure compliance with standards and best practices for responsible stewardship of digital information. Digital preservation strategies and actions address content creation, integrity and maintenance."⁷ This definition goes into further detail and discusses specificity of file formats and levels of preservation. This is to say that when you preserve digital content, you need to decide what file formats you will be preserving and to what level you will preserve—will you be offering basic, limited, or the highest level of digital preservation support, and for which file formats? This is a decision that is different for every organization and will take into consideration a multitude of factors, including funds, staff availability, and the accessibility of certain technologies. This long definition also states that what you should be addressing in your goal of digital preservation is content creation, integrity, and maintenance. Let us look at these three items in more detail.

Content Creation

This task involves such matters as "the production of reliable master files [and] sufficient descriptive, administrative, and structural metadata to ensure future access."⁸

Content creation makes certain that digital items are understandable and usable for current and future purposes. You must remember that it is not sufficient to only preserve the digital object—you must also preserve that object's metadata. Metadata can be defined as "information that characterizes another information resource, especially for purposes of documenting, describing, preserving or managing that resource."⁹

Content Integrity

This task requires items such as "documentation of all policies, strategies and procedures, recorded provenance and change history for all objects, verification mechanisms [and] routine audits."[10] Content integrity makes certain that digital items are accurate and complete through the use of checksums and fixity audits. The National Digital Stewardship Alliance defines a checksum as

> an algorithmically-computed numeric value for a file or a set of files used to validate the state and content of the file for the purpose of detecting accidental errors that may have been introduced during its transmission or storage. The integrity of the data can be checked at any later time by recomputing the checksum and comparing it with the stored one. If the checksums match, the data was almost certainly not altered.[11]

When you generate a current checksum and compare it to the originally created checksum, you are doing a fixity audit. There are many different checksum algorithms, the most common being CRC32, SHA-1, and MD5.[12] Checksum calculators are the tools used to compute checksums. There are plenty of checksum calculator programs available, each supporting a different algorithm. A quick internet search of "checksum calculator" will provide you with a variety of programs to download. If you are using a content management system (CMS) you will most likely be able to do a fixity check from within the CMS.

Content Maintenance

This task includes the "continuous monitoring and management of files, creation and testing of disaster prevention and recovery plans [and] periodic review and updating of policies and procedures."[13] It is crucial to understand that digital preservation is more than simply digitizing items and/or storing your digital items. It is an ongoing effort and, as mentioned previously, it requires much more maintenance than the preservation of physical or analog objects.

In short, the difference between digitization and digital preservation is that digitization makes content digital, but it will not preserve your digital objects and make sure of an accurate rendering of your digital content over time; that requires digital preservation. Digital preservation involves checksums, error detections, data storage, and data migration, all of which are going to assure your digital objects will be preserved for the long term.

DIGITAL PRESERVATION AND OAIS

The Open Archival Information System (OAIS) reference model is an international standard that provides a framework for the understanding of archival concepts needed for preserving digital data and documents over the long term. The term "open" in OAIS simply means that the model was developed in an open way. It is not meant to imply that access should be open or unrestricted. The OAIS model is so popular because it is like a road map that offers you a framework for long-term digital preservation. While the OAIS model is fairly adaptable and most institutions use this model, not everyone does; do not be afraid to seek an alternative model if you find OAIS does not work for you. The full OAIS model is available as a PDF online.

DEFINING DIGITAL CURATION

Digital curation can be defined as "the actions needed to maintain digital research data and other digital materials over their entire life cycle and over time for current and future generations of users."[14] The digital life cycle focuses on selection, metadata creation, access, and digital preservation. In other words, digitization and digital preservation are parts of digital curation. Your digital curation project will involve you selecting materials to digitize, accurately describing your digital objects, providing access to your digital objects, and then preserving those digital objects for the long term.

CONCLUSION

In this chapter you have learned the difference between digitization, digital preservation, and digital curation. Digitization is the reformatting of physical or analog materials to a digital format, while digital preservation is ensuring the long-term access of digital content over time. Digital curation involves both of these; digitization and digital preservation are simply parts of the digital life cycle. In terms of commitment, digitization is a process fixed in time, in which you digitally capture an object. Once (and if) you do it correctly, you are done and can move on to the next project. Digital preservation and digital curation, on the other hand, are an active, long-term commitment.[15] This chapter has also helped you understand the benefits of digitization and if digitization is right for your project. It is important to carefully examine your organization's needs and examine whether a digital curation project will meet those needs.

NOTES

1. Jennifer Howard, "Storm Damage at NYU Library Offers Lessons for Disaster Planning in the Stacks," *Chronicle of Higher Education* (November 23, 2012): A18–A19.
2. "Digitization of Local History Material," Monroe County Library System, Rochester Public Library - Central Library, accessed January 9, 2017, http://www3.libraryweb.org/central.aspx?id=228.
3. Victoria Billings, "The Japanese-American Digitization Project: Collaboration to Tell a Story," CSU Libraries Network, Council of Library Deans, January 20, 2015, http://libraries.calstate.edu/japanese-american-digitization-project/.
4. ALCTS Preservation and Reformatting Section, Working Group on Defining Digital Preservation, "Definitions of Digital Preservation," (ALA Annual Conference, Washington, DC, February 14, 2012), http://www.ala.org/alcts/resources/preserv/defdigpres0408.
5. ALCTS Preservation and Reformatting Section, "Definitions of Digital Preservation."
6. InterPARES 2 Project Terminology Database, accessed January 13, 2017, http://www.interpares.org/ip2/ip2_terminology_db.cfm.
7. ALCTS Preservation and Reformatting Section, "Definitions of Digital Preservation."
8. ALCTS Preservation and Reformatting Section, "Definitions of Digital Preservation."
9. InterPARES 2 Project Terminology Database.
10. ALCTS Preservation and Reformatting Section, "Definitions of Digital Preservation."
11. "Glossary," National Digital Stewardship Alliance, Digital Library Federation, accessed January 11, 2017, http://ndsa.org/glossary/.
12. Edward M. Corrado and Heather Moulaison Sandy, *Digital Preservation for Libraries, Archives, and Museums* (Lanham, MD: Rowman & Littlefield, 2014).
13. ALCTS Preservation and Reformatting Section, "Definitions of Digital Preservation."
14. N. Beagrie, "Digital Curation for Science, Digital Libraries, and Individuals," *International Journal of Digital Curation* 1, no. 1 (2006): 3–16.
15. Bill LeFurgy, "Digitization Is Different Than Digital Preservation: Help Prevent Digital Orphans!" *The Signal* (blog), Library of Congress, July 15, 2011, http://blogs.loc.gov/thesignal/2011/07/digitization-is-different-than-digital-preservation-help-prevent-digital-orphans/.

Chapter Two

What Every Project Needs to Get Started

Before getting started on your digital curation project, there are some important items you will need to prepare. First you need to come up with some selection criteria for choosing what to digitize. Based on those criteria you can then create a priority list for the objects you wish to digitize, making your project more manageable. You will then go ahead and create a digital preservation policy to help everyone involved in your project understand why and how you are going to undertake the preservation of your digital objects. You will also need to be prepared for any legal and ethical issues that might come your way, so you will need to document how your organization plans to handle these issues should they arise. More documentation is needed on metadata, specifically what kind of metadata you will create and what metadata standards you will use. You will then put all of this information together to form a digital collection policy. Finally, we will address how to fund your digital curation project through grants and community support.

CREATE SELECTION CRITERIA

Beginning a digital curation project involves choosing what objects to digitize. Though you may want to digitize everything, the reality of the matter is you will most likely not be able to, either due to time constraints, financial constraints, or a combination of the two. Therefore, you must decide what you are going to digitize, and the best way to do that is to evaluate your objects based on value, demand, condition, legal and ethical issues, and availability.

- Value: Does this object have historical and/or research value? Is the object unique or rare?
- Demand: Is this object in demand? Items in high demand are good candidates for digitization. If an item is not in high demand but you think digitization could attract enough viewers to justify the cost, then this item could be considered for digitization.[1]
- Condition of Materials: Is this object in fragile or stable condition? Fragile and/or deteriorating objects will have to have any conservation treatments completed before digitization can begin. Normally you may want to start with items in the best condition, because they will have a relatively easy and smooth digitization process; items in need of conservation will hold up your project. On the other hand, if you are considering digitization as a means of preservation, you may want to put very fragile items high on your priority list.
- Legal and Ethical Issues: Are there any legal and/or ethical issues involved with digitizing this object? Is this object under copyright protection? Do you have the time and energy to gain permission to digitize this object? Are there any privacy issues with the object you wish to digitize? Too many legal and ethical issues may persuade you to not move forward with digitizing an object.
- Availability: Is this object already available online? Before an item is digitized, always check to see if a digital copy already exists. Items that are already digitized should not be selected for digitization. The only exception would be if your digitization offered something new; perhaps your digital version is at a higher resolution rate, is in full color, or contains an interesting annotation.[2]

CREATE A PRIORITY LIST

Based on the above criteria you can create a priority list to help you select items for digitization. Your list should include the five criteria above, and a score between 1 and 3 should be given for each item. The higher the score, the higher the item should be on the priority list. See table 2.1 for more details.

CREATE A DIGITAL PRESERVATION POLICY

A digital preservation policy is a framework that helps explain the reasons your institution or organization is undertaking digital preservation and acts as a guideline for all who are involved in the organization's digital preservation plan. The policy should withstand staff changes and institutional transitions. The most successful digital preservation policy will be tailored to the organ-

Table 2.1. Priority List

Use the following rubric for each item you wish to digitize. For high quality objects, use the "Condition (High Quality Priority)" section of the table, and leave the other condition section blank. For more fragile objects, use the "Condition (Fragility Priority)" section of the table. The higher the item scores, the higher up it should be on the priority list.

	Score item on a scale of 1 to 3	Enter score here
Value	1 = Little to no value 2 = Some value 3 = High in value	
Demand	1 = This item is not in high demand 2 = This item has some demand 3 = This item is in high demand	
Condition (High Quality Priority)	1 = This item is very fragile 2 = This item is somewhat fragile 3 = This item is in very good condition	
Condition (Fragility Priority)	1 = This item is in very good condition 2 = This item is somewhat fragile 3 = This item is very fragile	
Legal and Ethical Issues	1 = There are many legal and ethical issues that need to be addressed. 2 = There are some legal and ethical issues that need to be addressed. 3 = There are no legal or ethical issues that need to be addressed.	
Availability	1 = Multiple sources have already placed this item online. 2 = One source has already placed this item online. 3 = This item is not currently available online.	

If your item scored:

5–10 points: It is a low priority item.

11–14 points: It is a medium priority item.

15–18 points: It is a high priority item.

Consider breaking down the digitization part of the project into the three priority phases and tackling each one at a time.

---

ization's specific needs, but while no two digital preservation policies are alike, the list below provides the most common elements that should be included in a policy.

1. Purpose. The benefits of long-term access to digital objects.

2. Objectives. What do you hope to achieve with your digital preservation program? What are your goals for organizing, managing, and undertaking preservation activities?
3. Scope. What type of material will the policy cover? Example: Our organization will only preserve born digital items.
4. Responsibilities. Define the roles and responsibilities of different staff members in general terms. When creating this section, list the department or the staff member (by title, not by personal name) and their responsibility. Example: Cataloging and Metadata Department will make certain that metadata is compliant with standards, best practices, and existing metadata policies.
5. Guidelines and Principles. These are general recommendations to help guide your preservation policy and strategy.

   a. Access. How will access be supported and how will it be provided?
   b. Authenticity. How will authenticity be established?
   c. Standards and Best Practices. What current standards and best practices will the organization follow in relation to the life cycle of the digital objects? You will most likely be using Open Archival Information System Reference Model (OAIS) and the PREMIS Data Dictionary for Preservation Metadata.
   d. Training. Will your organization provide ongoing training on digital preservation topics for staff members? Example: We are committed to providing continuing education on digital preservation topics for all staff/ select staff/senior staff, etc.

6. Policy Review. The digital preservation policy will need to be evaluated regularly to ensure that implemented strategies continue to support your organization's mission. How often will you review the policy and make updates? Example: We are committed to reviewing and updating the digital preservation policy every three years.
7. Preservation Strategy. How will you ensure that the content of your digital objects remains in a usable form over time? Your strategy should identify essential actions needed for active digital preservation. In the next section the preservation strategy will be discussed in more detail.

CHOOSING A DIGITAL PRESERVATION STRATEGY

When choosing a digital preservation strategy, the decision should be based on the needs of your particular project and the abilities of those involved in the digital preservation of these objects. We will discuss the two main strategies of migration and emulation, and highlight some advantages and disadvantages for each strategy.

Migration can be defined as "the process of moving or transferring digital objects from one system to another."[3] Migration can be performed as hardware migration or as software migration. Hardware migration involves copying digital objects from one generation or configuration of hardware to another. Software migration is the transferring of digital objects from one software application or file format to another. As with anything, there are pros and cons to the migration strategy. Migration may be a good option for you if your current items are being stored on CDs, USB flash drives, or any other sort of external storage medium. These types of external storage media are usually not suggested for long-term use, since the data can come to be inaccessible due to media and hardware obsolescence or degradation.

Migration is also advantageous because it is a widely used approach and processes for basic migration are well established, making it relatively easy for the digital preservation beginner. However, it is important to keep in mind that this strategy is not a one-time deal; in fact, migration needs to be repeated on a regular basis so it does require a large commitment of time. In an effort to save time some organizations may choose to only migrate items on request. This is a risky decision, because migration may not be possible by the time an item is requested. In addition, another disadvantage is the prospect of some of the data or attributes (e.g., formatting) of the digital object becoming lost during migration, possibly compromising the authenticity of the record. A final disadvantage to mention is that the look or feel of the original is not necessarily replicated with the migration method. For this reason, some may choose to use emulation as their digital preservation approach instead.

Emulation is "the reproduction of the behavior and results of obsolete software or systems through the development of new hardware and/or software to allow execution of the old software or systems on future computers."[4] In other words, emulation is a method in which you recreate the behavior of one computer on another computer. With emulation, the focus is on the technological environment in which the object was created, while with migration the focus is on the digital object itself.

Emulation can be applied to applications, operating systems, or hardware. When you perform application emulation you create a new software application that can do what an earlier application did, to allow the files to be read. Operating systems emulation involves allowing all the software that ran on the old platform to run on the new emulated version. If you choose to emulate an operating system you will need a suitable hardware platform. Hardware emulation consists of creating a new emulated platform that can run all the operating systems and applications that ran on the original hardware platform. This is to say that all the operating systems and applications that ran on the original hardware platform are able to run devoid of modification on the new, emulated platform. This approach makes the emulation of applications and operating systems unnecessary, since they are capable of being preserved in their original state and run on the emulated hardware.

As with migration, there are both advantages and disadvantages to using emulation as your digital preservation strategy. One of the biggest advantages is that emulation involves a one-time effort for a sizable collection of digital objects. This is because, as mentioned previously, the focus is on emulating the technology used to access the digital object, not the digital object itself. Emulation allows the original file to maintain its accessibility and minimizes the risk of data loss that may occur with repeated migration cycles.

Disadvantages of emulation include patent and licensing issues, cost, and the fact that it can be technologically challenging for many. Emulation involves technological skills that the average person does not have; you will need to hire someone or train your staff to write emulator code. It is important to note that most emulation methods will consist of preserving or emulating proprietary software, which is covered by patent, license, or other intellectual property rights. This will possibly open a whole can of worms that your organization may not want to or cannot deal with. Then there are the high initial costs involved in emulation; if your organization will not be able to fund this strategy in the long-term, it may be wise to choose a different approach.

As mentioned previously, migration and emulation are the most common digital preservation approaches, but they are not the only strategies available. One other strategy of digital preservation is known as technology preservation. It is based on preserving the technical environment that runs the system, such as operating systems, original application software, and media drives. It is sometimes referred to as the "computer museum" solution or the "hardware museum" solution. Maintenance is almost impossible under this strategy, because keeping obsolete technology in usable form necessitates a sizable investment in equipment and personnel. This strategy may be an adequate short-term solution but it is not a practicable approach for long-term digital preservation.

There is also the concept of data archaeology, which involves recovering computer data from now obsolete media or formats. This strategy may also be known as digital archaeology or data recovery, though it is important to note that data recovery merely means the recovery of data while data archaeology refers to recovery and restoration of readability and usability. Because this strategy is labor intensive and technically challenging (you will most likely have to employ a trained specialist for it), data archaeology should only be used as an emergency recovery strategy.

One final digital preservation strategy we will discuss is bitstream preservation. Bitstream preservation, or bitstream copying, is probably the most well-known preservation strategy to the digital preservation beginner, though you probably just call it "backing up your data." When you back up your data you are making an exact duplicate of a digital object onto another type of storage medium. Backing up your data is essential, but it is not a strategy on its own; it should be used in combination with another digital preservation approach. Bitstream preservation only preserves your digital objects from hardware and media failure; it will not preserve your items from digital obsolescence.

Now that we have completed an overview of the most common digital preservation approaches, you must select which one(s) you will use in your policy. Below are some suggested criteria to consider when choosing the digital preservation approach best suited to your project and your organization. Kenneth Thibodeau, former director of the Electronic Records Archives Program at the National Archives and Records Administration (NARA), recommends the following four criteria:

1. Feasibility: Do you have or can you acquire the required hardware and software of the chosen approach?
2. Sustainability: Can this approach be applied now and into the foreseeable future? If not, is there an alternative direction to take if or when this current approach stops being viable?
3. Practicality: Is this approach practical? Is the cost of this approach practical for your organization? Is the required skill set for this approach practical for your staff?
4. Appropriateness: Does this approach work for the particular types of digital objects to be preserved?

These four criteria are an excellent guideline to help your organization select a digital preservation approach that works for the projects you want to undertake. Your digital preservation strategy will also need to address the life cycle management of your digital objects. This strategy includes the following:

a. Creation. Will the digital content you create follow current standards and best practices for capture and formatting?

b. Selection. How will you decide on selecting items? Example: Selection for digital preservation will be done in coordination with existing collection development policies.
c. Ingest. How will you handle the ingest of materials into the collection? What guidelines will you follow for ingest procedures?
d. Metadata Creation. What is the procedure for creating metadata? Will your organization include administrative, technical, structural, and provenance metadata? Example: All digital resources created by (organization name) will adhere to our pending metadata policy.
e. Storage. How will you store your digital objects? You will need to think about the storage of such infrastructure as hardware, software, data backup, and more.
f. Access and Use. How will you ensure that your digital files are accessible in the long-term? Example: Digital objects and collections will be regularly reviewed and managed to ensure that files are accessible in the future.
g. Preservation Management. You will need to lay out detailed procedures and workflows for preservation actions.
h. Deselection. How will you decide when and what digital objects to deselect from your collection? Example: Digital objects will be assessed, examined, and disposed of as needed, based on current collection development policies.

CHALLENGES AND THREATS TO DIGITAL PRESERVATION

When creating your digital preservation policy and strategy, it is important to understand the biggest challenges to digital preservation. The main challenges can be narrowed down to incomplete or inadequate capture and obsolescence. Careful monitoring of the digitization process can mitigate inadequate capture, and a comprehensive digital preservation plan can help you avoid obsolescence. You must also be aware of the physical threats of digital preservation. These include mostly storage and handling issues. The most common reason for untimely media failure is improper storage; therefore, it is important to maintain proper storage practices as well as temperature and relative humidity levels.[5] Use the Specific Storage Guidelines table (table 2.2) for reference when storing items, and use the Handling Guidelines tables (see tables 2.3, 2.4, and 2.5) for reference when handling magnetic and optical formats as well as flash media.

COPYRIGHT AND INTELLECTUAL PROPERTY DECISIONS

You will need to have a policy detailing how you will address any copyright and intellectual property decisions that may come up when digitizing an object. Use the Copyright and Intellectual Property Decisions Flowchart (figure 2.1) for guidance.

CREATE METADATA DOCUMENTATION

Metadata is a term for structured information that helps with the discovery of resources. This information "describes, explains, locates, or otherwise makes it easier to retrieve, use, or manage an information resource."[6] Metadata is composed of a number of elements, which are categorized based on the different functions they support.[7] The three basic categories of metadata are descriptive, technical, and administrative.[8]

Descriptive Metadata

Descriptive metadata is used to help us describe and identify resources. This type of metadata can allow us to properly search for and retrieve resources through a catalog or through the World Wide Web.[9] An example of this is

Table 2.2. Specific Storage Guidelines

Media	Temperature (in °F)	Relative Humidity (RH)	Storage Recommendations
Magnetic Formats	Between 62 and 70	30–45%	• Store upright • Enclose media in container made of archival quality materials • Do not pack items tightly
Optical and Magneto-Optical Formats	Between 62 and 70	35–50%	• Store upright in rigid cases • Remove any paper inserts
Flash Storage	Between 62 and 70	30–45%	• Store flat • Do not store uncovered

Adapted from *The Preservation Management Handbook: A 21st-Century Guide for Libraries, Archives, and Museums*, by Ross Harvey and Martha R. Mahard (Lanham, MD: Rowman & Littlefield, 2014).

Table 2.3. Handling Guidelines for Magnetic Formats

Guidelines	Staff	Users
Clean and dry hands before handling media.		
Avoid sudden temperature changes.		
Do not touch the magnetic recording surface.		
Never read media without a write blocker in place.		
Never leave media in a drive after use.		

Adapted from *The Preservation Management Handbook: A 21st-Century Guide for Libraries, Archives, and Museums*, by Ross Harvey and Martha R. Mahard (Lanham, MD: Rowman & Littlefield, 2014).

being able to search an organization's image collection via a catalog to find photos of dogs, or using an internet search engine to look up photos of cats; the results you receive are there because they have the proper descriptive metadata attached to them.

Technical Metadata

Technical or structural metadata is used to provide information about the internal structure of resources. This type of metadata includes information on file types, file formats, and file size.[10]

Administrative Metadata

Administrative metadata is used to manage and preserve resources. This metadata indicates information such as when and how the resource was created, the file type and other technical information, and who can access the resource.[11] There are also two subsets of administrative data:

- Rights Management Metadata: This metadata focuses on intellectual property rights such as copyrights, user restrictions, and license agreements.[12]
- Preservation Metadata: This metadata provides the information needed to carry out the preservation and access of resources. It also establishes the authenticity of digital content, and records the chain of custody and provenance for a digital resource.[13]

You will want to document what metadata you will be collecting and what metadata standard(s) you will use for your digital collection(s).

Table 2.4. Handling Guidelines for Optical Formats

Guidelines	Staff	Users
Clean and dry hands before handling media.		
Handle discs by the outer edge or the center hole.		
Do not touch the writable side or the label side of the disc unnecessarily.		
Only use solvent-free, water-based markers for labeling.		
Never leave in a drive after use.		
Check media for delamination and information loss at least annually.		

Adapted from *The Preservation Management Handbook: A 21st-Century Guide for Libraries, Archives, and Museums*, by Ross Harvey and Martha R. Mahard (Lanham, MD: Rowman & Littlefield, 2014).

CREATE A DIGITAL COLLECTION POLICY

Your institution may already have a collection development policy, but you will need to create one specifically for digital collections. Here are some guidelines on what you will need to draft a digital collection policy:

1. Mission: List your organization's mission statement.
2. Scope: List materials to be considered under this policy.
3. Access: List who has access to the materials, and list any materials that may have restrictions on access and/or usage.
4. Preservation: Place your digital preservation policy here.
5. Policy Review: List how often faculty or staff will review this policy.
6. Selection Criteria: List a set of guiding values to aid in the selection of material. You can use the ones put forth at the beginning of this chapter or you can create your own.
7. Copyright and Intellectual Property Guidelines: Detail how you will handle copyright and intellectual property issues. Include Copyright and Intellectual Property Decisions Flowchart (figure 2.1) here if desired.
8. Metadata Standards: Detail what metadata work is needed to support the collections. The metadata documentation discussed earlier in this chapter will go here.
9. Withdrawal Policy/Takedown Policy: List a person for users to contact should they have questions or wish to contest the inclusion of specific digital objects. See box for Takedown Policy Sample.

Table 2.5. Handling Guidelines for Flash Media

Guidelines	Staff	Users
Never read media without a write blocker in place.		
Never leave a drive attached to a machine after use.		
Never remove a flash drive from the USB port while it is still in operation.		
When not in use, make sure the flash drive's USB connector is covered with a cap.		

Adapted from *The Preservation Management Handbook: A 21st-Century Guide for Libraries, Archives, and Museums*, by Ross Harvey and Martha R. Mahard (Lanham, MD: Rowman & Littlefield, 2014).

TAKEDOWN POLICY SAMPLE

If you are a rights holder and are concerned that you have found material on the (Institution's Name) Digital Collections Website without your permission and believe our inclusion of this material on our website violates your rights (e.g., inclusion is not covered by Fair Use or other exemption to a copyright holder's rights), please contact us and include the following:

- Your contact information, such as an address, telephone number, and email address
- Exact URL where you found the material
- Details that describe the material (title, collection name, number of items, etc.)
- The reason why you believe that your rights have been violated, with any pertinent documentation
- If your complaint concerns intellectual property rights, confirmation that you are the rights holder, or an authorized representative of the rights holder
- If your complaint concerns libel, defamation, confidentiality or personal data, confirmation that you are either the publisher or the subject of the material in question, or their authorized representative

Upon receipt of a request, staff of (Institution's Name) will:

- Promptly acknowledge the request via email, or other means of communication if you do not have an email account.
- Assess the validity of the request.

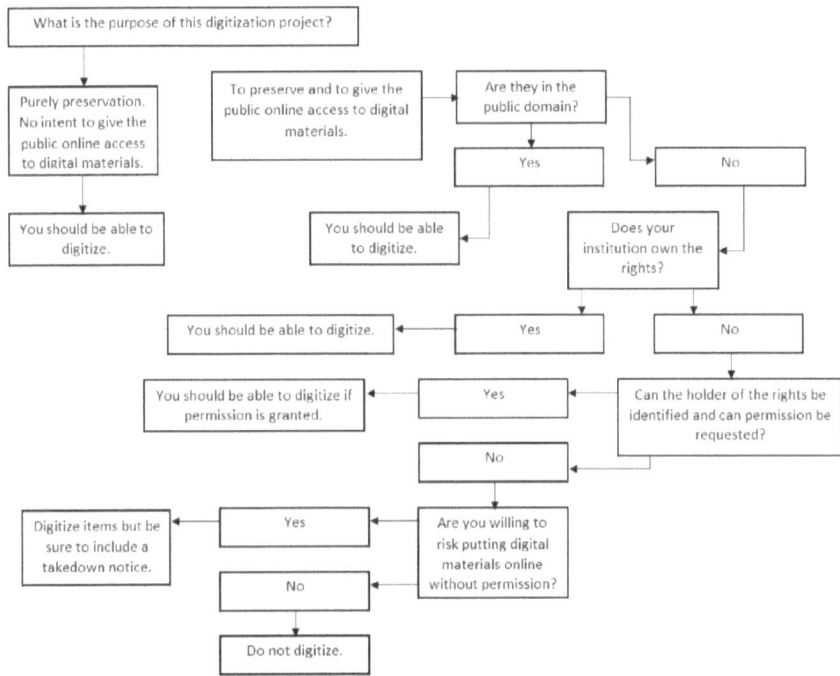

Figure 2.1. Copyright and Intellectual Property Decisions Flowchart Adapted from Gertz, Janet. "Should You? May You? Can You? Factors in Selecting Rare Books and Special Collections for Digitization." *Info Today* **(March 2013).**

- Upon request, we may temporarily remove the material from public view while we assess the concern.
- Upon completion of the assessment, we will take appropriate action and communicate that action to you.
- If (Institution's Name) is not able to determine that it is permitted to provide access to the work(s) in question, we will cease providing access to the work(s).

When creating your digital collection policy, you can also use the National Information Standards Organization (NISO) guidelines for creating good collections. NISO has put together nine principles that they consider attributes of a good digital collection. Let's look at them in detail:

- Collection Principle #1: A good digital collection is created according to an explicit collection development policy.

Explanation: A good collection aligns with your digital collection development policy. This means the intended digital collection should be an overall fit with your organization's policy. Note: Your institution may already have a collection development policy, but you will need to create one specifically for digital collections.

- Collection Principle #2: Collections should be described, so that a user can discover characteristics of the collection, including scope, format, restrictions on access, ownership, and any information significant for determining the collection's authenticity, integrity, and interpretation.

  Explanation: Your digital collections need to be described in a way that allows users to discover the existence of the collection and also helps them to comprehend what they are viewing.[14] In other words, a good collection has good metadata.

- Collection Principle #3: A good collection is curated, which is to say, its resources are actively managed during their life cycle.

  Explanation: You need to be able to manage this collection for its entire lifecycle. This means that when you choose a digital collection you should make certain that you can not only digitize the collection but also continue to provide access it, and that you can properly preserve the collection as well.

- Collections Principle #4: A good collection is broadly available and avoids unnecessary impediments to use. Collections should be accessible to persons with disabilities and effectively usable in conjunction with adaptive technologies.

  Explanation: Can you make certain that your digital collection is available, easy to use, and accessible? A good digital collection's web pages and search forms will be functional on various browsers and various versions of those browsers.[15] You should also regularly test your collection's access points on different operating systems, and look for any issues with screen resolution, color variations, and display of non-English language characters.[16]

- Collections Principle #5: A good collection respects intellectual property rights.

  Explanation: Are there any intellectual property rights that prevent you from digitizing and making your collection accessible? If so, you most likely will not be able to digitize this collection.

- Collections Principle #6: A good collection has mechanisms to supply usage data and other data that allows standardized measures of usefulness to be recorded.

  Explanation: Your digital collection needs to be useful. The definition of "useful" will vary based on your organization's focus. Ideally you will collect both quantitative and qualitative data, like usage statistics or user feedback surveys, for your collection.

- Collections Principle #7: A good collection is interoperable.

  Explanation: When it is said that a good collection is interoperable, this means that your digital collection should not be isolated unto itself. A digital collection that is interoperable shares its metadata with external search engines.
- Collections Principle #8: A good collection integrates into the workflows of staff and end users.

  Explanation: When beginning your digital curation project, you want to look for ways that you can integrate the required tasks of staff into already existing workflows. For end users, look at the research tools they are currently using and try to integrate your new digital collection with those tools, making it easier for them to find and use your collection.
- Collections Principle #9: A good collection is sustainable over time.

  Explanation: A sustainable digital collection has regular maintenance. Examples include having access points regularly checked to make sure they are still usable, and making sure that all software and hardware are updated as needed.[17]

FUNDING YOUR DIGITAL CURATION PROJECT

We live in a time of ever-changing priorities and dwindling budgets, and obtaining funds for digitization and digital preservation activities can be quite a challenge. Maintaining digital data for the long term is not a one-shot deal; it requires continued activity and it needs a dedicated budget. Unfortunately, many institutions and organizations do not have the necessary funding for a digital curation project. Fortunately, federal and state agencies, foundations, and corporations offer grant programs for both digitization and preservation. It must be noted that these sources can be extremely competitive, so it is important that you stand out from the crowd when applying for funding. Below are some ideas to help you when you are seeking funding for your project:

1. Can you clearly articulate your need? You need to be able not only to articulate your need but to do it concisely. This is where the elevator speech comes in handy. The elevator speech is where you clearly explain your organization's mission in 30 seconds or less (or the time it would take you to ride in an elevator with your potential funder). This is important, because you often have only a short window of opportunity to get your point across to a potential institutional funder or individual donor, and you do not want to waste this precious moment. There are several key components of an effective elevator speech. However, there is often quite a bit of homework and research

that goes into that 30-second pitch. The bottom line is that you must know who you are, because the elevator speech is just the tip of the iceberg. Here is what you should include in your elevator speech:

    a. Mission
    b. Your Demographic
    c. Problem Statement
    d. Your Goals
    e. The Pitch for the Project

You must have a clear, focused, and well-articulated mission. You must know who your target demographic is. You must define and understand the problem you are working to solve, and you must know what you want to achieve and how you will achieve it.

2. Have you considered all aspects of your need? Are you including all staffing, equipment, and time needed for your digital curation project?
3. Do you have measurable goals? Is your plan well thought out, with achievable milestones?
4. What is the outcome of your project? What will be better, different, or new after you finish your project?

You will also have an edge on your competition if you take time to research your potential funders. Begin by compiling a list of foundations, organizations, and other funders whose program interests might lead them to support your organization and the specific projects for which you are seeking funding. Try to be inclusive at this stage. If you think a specific donor or foundation should go on the list, go ahead and include it. As you learn of new prospective funders, it is a good idea to keep track of basic information about them. That way, when a new project comes up, you can immediately identify potential funders. Track their policies for giving and look to see if they have funded projects similar to yours in the past; if they have, then your project might just be a good fit for them. You can read up on their focus areas and recent giving. You can find this information easily by reviewing their 990s. A good resource for finding 990s is http://foundationcenter.org/find-funding/990-finder.

It is important not to forget the power of networking; become a member of museums and local organizations, and go to functions. Once you have found potential funders, you can send them letters to see if you are a good match for their foundation. To save you time and effort, know the limits for support before you apply. There is no point in applying for something that the foundation cannot grant you because you do not meet their criteria. Limits can include type of program funded, geographical area, and minimum/maximum funding the foundation will grant. That is not always public, but find out ahead of time about these limits if you can. It will help you decide how much to ask for.

Another thing you can do to edge out your competition is to seek out a mentor. Ask a trusted colleague who is good at writing grants about his or her experiences. This colleague can help you write out some talking points or rehearse the conversation. They can even sit with you while you make the preliminary call. The preliminary call is when you call up the potential grant funder and tell them a bit about your project (see the elevator speech above) and inquire whether your project would be a good fit for their grant. Do not be afraid to make this phone call; you are not bothering the funder. Funders would actually prefer that you make this preliminary contact, as it saves you and them time. If you reach out to funders before submitting your proposal, they will not have to read a grant proposal that is not applicable to their grant. You should schedule a time to make the call, because if you do not schedule a time to make it happen you will most likely put it off indefinitely. If you get a voicemail message when you make the call, leave a message that includes a phone number where you can be reached easily, and always follow up. Make sure to record notes in your files, and to send any information requested promptly.

Beyond applying for a grant, you can also look to your community for support. Crowdfunding is a great way to raise funds for your project, and many libraries, archives, and museums have been using this method to support various projects. Kickstarter and Indiegogo are two of the more popular crowdfunding websites. Kickstarter will release funds only after the campaign reaches its funding goal, while Indiegogo allows you to choose between receiving funding as it comes in or waiting to see if you hit your target. Whichever platform you choose, be sure to promote your crowdfunding campaign. Promotional ideas include posting about your campaign on social media, via e-newsletters, and on the front page of your website. You may also want to consider reaching out to local media to bring awareness to your campaign.

CONCLUSION

In this chapter you learned that is important to document how to choose items for digitization, how to handle legal issues, and what types of metadata to collect, in addition to creating a digital preservation policy. All of this information will be extremely helpful for everyone currently involved in your project and those who might join the project at a later date. You also now know how to go about getting funding to make your digital curation project a reality.

NOTES

1. Janet Gertz, "Should You? May You? Can You? Factors in Selecting Rare Books and Special Collections for Digitization," *Computers in Libraries* (March 1, 2013).
2. Gertz, "Factors in Selecting Rare Books."
3. "InterPARES Project: Terminology Database." http://www.interpares.org/ip2/ip2_terminology_db.cfm.
4. "InterPARES Project: Terminology Database." http://www.interpares.org/ip2/ip2_terminology_db.cfm.
5. "Digital Preservation Management: Implementing Short-Term Strategies for Long-Term Problems," Cornell University Library, accessed July 1, 2017, http://www.dpworkshop.org/dpm-eng/oldmedia/threats.html.
6. National Information Standards Organization (NISO), "NISO Publishes 'Understanding Metadata' Primer," accessed April 20, 2017, http://www.niso.org/news/pr/view?item_key=163cc4576827006ed5adf7ef3b359416c4d94e15.
7. Sarah Higgins, "What Are Metadata Standards," Digital Curation Centre, February 2007, http://www.dcc.ac.uk/resources/briefing-papers/standards-watch-papers/what-are-metadata-standards.
8. Higgins, "What Are Metadata Standards."
9. NISO, "NISO Publishes 'Understanding Metadata' Primer," accessed April 20, 2017, http://www.niso.org/news/pr/view?item_key=163cc4576827006ed5adf7ef3b359416c4d94e15.
10. Edward M. Corrado and Heather Moulaison Sandy, *Digital Preservation for Libraries, Archives, and Museums* (Lanham: Rowman & Littlefield, 2014).
11. Corrado and Sandy, *Digital Preservation for Libraries*.
12. "Glossary," National Digital Stewardship Alliance, Digital Library Federation, accessed April 7, 2017, http://ndsa.org/glossary/.
13. "Glossary," National Digital Stewardship Alliance.
14. "Introduction," *Framework of Guidance for Building Good Digital Collections*, National Information Standards Organization, accessed June 20, 2017, http://framework.niso.org/.
15. "Collections Principle 4," National Information Standards Organization, last updated April 17, 2008, http://framework.niso.org/12.html.
16. "Collections Principle 4," National Information Standards Organization.
17. "Collections Principle 9," National Information Standards Organization, last updated September 3, 2008, http://framework.niso.org//17.html.

Part II

Digital Curation Projects Step-By-Step

Chapter Three

General Guidelines

In this chapter we will discuss the general guidelines that will be applicable to all your digital curation projects. We begin by recapping the criteria for choosing objects to digitize, then we discuss the equipment you will need for digitization, general guidelines for digitizing your chosen objects, how to accurately describe the objects and collection, how to provide access to your collection, and how to preserve your analog and digital objects.

DIGITIZATION

If your objects are not born digital, you will need to digitize them. Digitizing objects requires the right equipment, the appropriate amount of physical and digital space to accomplish this task, and documentation of the digitization. Let's look at these in depth:

Choosing What to Digitize

Before you begin the digitization process you must choose what to digitize. In chapter 2, we discussed five criteria for selecting items for digitization. Here is a quick recap:

1. Value
2. Demand
3. Condition of Materials
4. Legal and Ethical Issues
5. Availability

Choosing Equipment

The first step to digitization is to have the right equipment. This means that you have appropriate hardware and software that work for the type of objects you are digitizing.

Equipment Checklist

- All necessary hardware has been purchased.
- All hardware needing repair has been repaired or replaced.
- A list has been prepared with vendors to contact, should repairs be needed at a later time.
- All necessary software has been purchased.

Space Requirements

You will need to make certain that you have enough physical space to undertake this project.

Physical Space Checklist

- Sufficient space for computers
- Sufficient space for digitization equipment
- Sufficient space to lay out physical materials
- Sufficient space to store physical materials

Digital Storage Space

Just as you need to make sure adequate storage space is provided for physical objects, you need to make certain that you have sufficient storage space for digital objects.

Digital Storage Checklist

- Sufficient digital storage space for archival master files
- Sufficient digital storage space for access copies of files
- Three copies of each digital file, saved on two different media formats, and at least one copy backed up off site

Digitization Log

It is important to keep a log of what is being digitized. Each person performing the digitization of any objects should complete a log. Table 3.1 is an example of a log.

Digitization Workflow

In-House Digitization

With so many steps involved in digitization, it is strongly suggested that you create a workflow to allow for a smoother and easier process. A workflow can be described as a sequence of connected, repeatable steps that allow an activity to be completed from start to finish. Workflows are not a one size fits all deal, so make sure to tailor your workflow to your project and organization's needs. See table 3.2 below for an example of an in-house digitization workflow that will help guide you in establishing your own workflow.

Outsourcing Digitization

If your organization is choosing to outsource digitization, you will want to make sure you are choosing a reliable vendor that suits your needs. Consult with at least three vendors before making a decision, and ask them the following questions to aid in finalizing a vendor:

- Has the vendor ever digitized the type of material you want to digitize?
   Make sure that the vendor has experience with the materials you wish to digitize. Ask for referrals, if possible.
- What type of equipment does the vendor use (including scanners, digital cameras, and computers)?
   If you have fragile materials, you will want to make certain that the vendor does not use document feeders, which can damage your objects.
- What type of media does the vendor use for file storage?
   Inquire as to what type of media your objects will be stored on. Make sure the type of media is usable by your institution.
- What type of metadata does the vendor create for image files?
   It will be easier if you can get the vendor to create metadata for your digital objects. Find out what metadata standards they use to ensure you are getting metadata that is suited to your project.
- Who owns the files, you or the vendor?
   Make sure that you (and not the vendor) own the final product.

Table 3.1. Digitization Log

What is being digitized?
By whom?
Date(s) of digitization
What files were created?
Where are the files stored?

Table 3.2. In-House Digitization Workflow Example

Step 1: Preparation of Physical Objects	• Pull box of physical items. • If an item appears to be problematic (fragile, etc.), ask for guidance on how to proceed, if at all, with the item. • Boxes will be returned upon completion of scanning and quality control.
Step 2: Preparation of Digital Equipment	• All digitization equipment should be checked before digitization begins.
Step 3: Analog to Digital Conversion	• Upload digital objects from the local drive to your preferred network drive. • After verifying upload success, delete corresponding scans off local drive. • Upon completion of box, begin scanning the next box assigned to you.
Step 4: Quality Control	Physical Quality Control: • Verify all physical box content is present. • Check physical folder sequence numbers to check for gaps, etc. Digital Quality Control: • Check for correct file names and make all corrections necessary. • Check for count of scans by item level. • Spot-check that the scan of every 20th object is of the correct physical item, and spot-check these scans for quality. Make all corrections necessary.

- Where are the collections stored while at the vendor's facility?

  The storage area should be temperature controlled, without extreme fluctuations in either temperature or relative humidity.
- What type of security is available?

  The vendor should have adequate security measures in place to ensure that your materials are safe.
- What responsibility (if any) will the vendor assume if your collection is damaged while at its facility?

  This is important in case of natural or man-made disasters. If the vendor takes no responsibility, is this a risk you are willing to take?

Creating Good Digital Objects

It is important to remember that it is not enough to simply create digital objects for your project; you will want to make sure you are creating good objects. The National Information Standards Organization (NISO) has come up with six object principles to guide you in creating good digital objects:

- Object Principle #1: A good object exists in a format that supports its intended current and future use.
  Explanation: Your digital object should be able to migrate across platforms, be broadly accessible, and be formatted according to a recognized standard or best practice.[1]
- Object Principle #2: A good object is preservable.
  Explanation: A digital object is preservable when it does not create unnecessary barriers to accessibility over time, regardless of changing technologies.
- Object Principle #3: A good object is meaningful and useful outside of its local context.
  Explanation: Your digital object needs to be both portable and self-explanatory.[2] This means your digital object should be accessible and usable beyond the local level, and that ideally, the object's metadata is self-contained and the format choice of the object should be obvious to anyone accessing it.
- Object Principle #4: A good object will be named with a persistent, globally unique identifier that can be resolved to the current address of the object.
  Explanation: Your digital object needs to be named in such a way that it is unique, so it is easy to find, and your file-naming convention should be consistent. We will go into more detail on file naming later in this chapter.
- Object Principle #5: A good object can be authenticated.
  Explanation: It is important that your digital object can be authenticated. As you remember from chapter 1 of this book, authenticity refers to the trustworthiness of a record; is the record what it claims to be? Has the object been altered, and if so, when and by whom? Fixity checking, or fixity auditing, was also discussed as a means of checking content integrity, but other methods like digital watermarking and documentation of digital provenance (which can be recorded as metadata) can also help you determine a digital object's authenticity.[3]
- Object Principle #6: A good object has associated metadata.
  Explanation: Your digital object also needs to have a sufficient amount of associated metadata, either embedded within the object or stored separately and linked to the object described.[4]

Chapter 3

DESCRIBING THE COLLECTIONS

Recording Your Metadata

There are various ways you may choose to record your metadata. The most common ways of recording metadata are through spreadsheets, web forms, databases, or Extensible Markup Language (XML). Keep in mind that there is no one set system, so choose the one that works best for your organization.

Using Microsoft Excel to create spreadsheets containing metadata might be the simplest way to record your metadata, since most people are already familiar with Microsoft Excel (see figure 3.1).

Create one Excel file for each collection, with one row of metadata for each object. Many metadata fields (such as collection name and rights) will be repeated for each item you are listing. If you see that the data in a particular field will be repeated, it may be easier to copy the contents of the cell into all subsequent rows of metadata.[5] You might also have the option of using a web form to record all your metadata. You may also choose to use a database, and depending on the database you choose, you may be able to record your metadata directly into the database. If you had previously used an Excel spreadsheet to record your metadata, you may be able to convert it into a

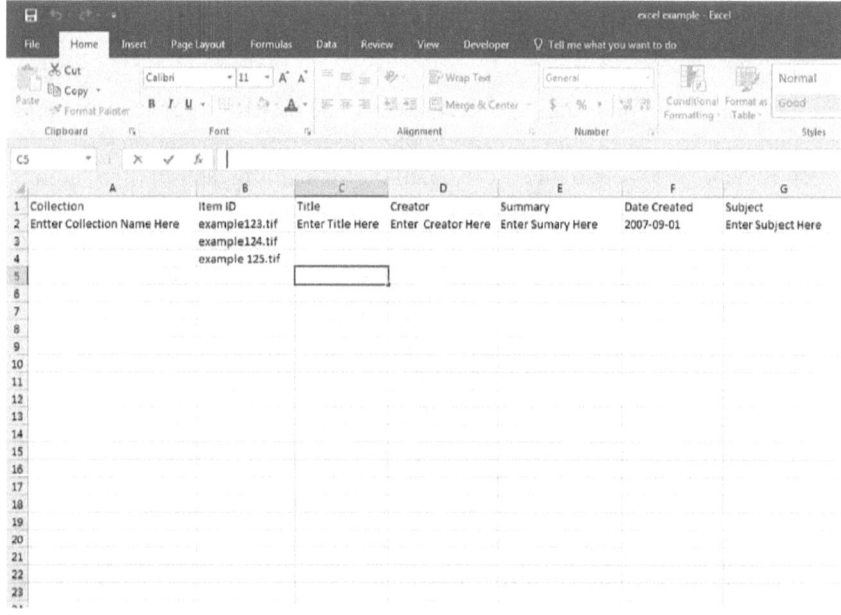

Figure 3.1. Recording Your Metadata: Spreadsheet Example

database with some minor revisions. Finally, you can also use Extensible Markup Language (XML) to record your metadata.

File Naming

Here are some general guidelines for naming your files:

- Guideline #1: The file name should be clear and concise, yet include sufficiently descriptive information, independent of where it is stored.
  Files are frequently copied to other folders, downloaded, and emailed. It is important to ensure that the file name, independent of the folder where the original file lives, is sufficiently descriptive.
  If the minutes document for the Digital Reformatting Work Group is stored in the folder labeled J:\working groups\Committees\Digital Reformatting\AgendasMinutes\DRWG-2014\, and is named "Minutes-20140103.docx," if moved it loses the context that it is the minutes for the Digital Reformatting Work Group. A more appropriate file name would be "Minutes-DRWG-20140103.docx."
- Guideline #2: DO NOT use special characters in a file name. Examples include the following symbols: \ / : * ? " > < | [ ] & $, .
  The characters listed above are frequently used for specific tasks in an electronic environment. For example, a forward slash is used to identify folder levels in Microsoft products, while Mac operating systems use the colon. Periods are used in front of file-name extensions to denote file formats such as .jpg and .doc; using them in a file name could result in lost files or errors.
- Guideline #3: Use hyphens instead of periods, underscores, or spaces.
  As mentioned above, periods already have a specific function in a file name, which is to tell the computer program where the file-name extension begins. Spaces are frequently translated in a Web environment to be read as "%20," and underscores are lost in hyperlinking and underlining.
  For example: The document "File-Naming-Convention-20150810.docx" contains hyphens, because if spaces were used, as in "File Naming Convention 20150810.docx," the document name would appear as "File%20Naming%20Convention%2020150810.docx."
  If underscores were used, as in "File_Naming_Convention_20150810.docx," the underscores would disappear when underlined or hyperlinked, as File Naming Convention 20150810.docx.
- Guideline #4: Being consistent will allow the most effective search and retrieval over time.
  Do:

   a. Minutes-Web-Governance-Committee-20150113.docx

b. Minutes-Web-Governance-Committee-20150217.docx
   c. Minutes-Web-Governance-Committee-20150317.docx

Don't:

   a. Minutes-Web-Gov-Committee-20150113.docx
   b. Minutes-WebGovernance-20150113.docx
   c. Minutes-WG-Committee-20150113.docx

- Guideline #5: When including a number in a file name, always give it as a two-digit number rather than a one-digit number.

    To maintain the numeric order when file names include numbers, it is important to include the zero for numbers 0–9. This helps to retrieve the latest record number (i.e., 01, 02, . . . 99), unless it is a year or another number with more than two digits.

    Done correctly your files will look like this:

    a. OfficeProceduresV01
    b. OfficeProceduresV02
    c. OfficeProceduresV03
    d. OfficeProceduresV04
    e. OfficeProceduresV05
    f. OfficeProceduresV06
    g. OfficeProceduresV07
    h. OfficeProceduresV08
    i. OfficeProceduresV09
    j. OfficeProceduresV10

    Done incorrectly your files will look like this:

    a. OfficeProceduresV1
    b. OfficeProceduresV10
    c. OfficeProceduresV2
    d. OfficeProceduresV39
    e. OfficeProceduresV4
    f. OfficeProceduresV5
    g. OfficeProceduresV6
    h. OfficeProceduresV7
    i. OfficeProceduresV8
    j. OfficeProceduresV9

If you are not creating files from scratch and find yourself needing to rename many files in order to comply with best practices, try using these file naming applications: Bulk Rename Utility (Windows) or Renamer (Mac).

Choosing a Metadata Standard

When deciding on what metadata standard to use for your collection, you need to think about what metadata standard works best for the objects you are describing. Some metadata sets work better for particular collections than others. Some metadata standards can be more complicated than others, so it is important that those involved in this project have the skill set to work with a particular standard. For example, the vast majority of projects choose Dublin Core because it is very basic and easy to learn.

You may also want to consider the following list of questions compiled by NISO to help in the decision process.

1. What is the purpose of the digital collection?
2. What are the goals and objectives for building this collection?
3. Who are the targeted users? What information do they need, and what is their typical information-seeking behavior?
4. Will the materials be accessed at the collection level, as individual items, or both?
5. Do multiple versions or manifestations of the object need to be distinguished from each other?
6. Will the collection or its objects have metadata before the digital collection is built?
7. What subject discipline will be involved? What are the metadata standards commonly used within this discipline?
8. What metadata standards are used by organizations in this domain? Which ones are most appropriate for this particular collection?
9. How rich a description is needed, and does the metadata need to convey hierarchical relationships?[6]

Documenting Your Metadata

When you decide on a metadata standard you will need to give documentation for each element and attribute. Simply give a description of what this field should be used for and define how to formulate the data. Let's look at Dublin Core as an example:

Title, Date, and Creator are three elements in Dublin Core.

- Title: Detail how one should properly format a title.

- *Example:* For a formal title, transcribe it as it appears on the source of information.
- Date: Detail how one should properly format a date.
  Example: We will use ISO8501 best practice for dates: YYYY–MM–DD.
- Creator: Detail how one should properly format the creator.
  Example: Creator's name should be written as last name, first name, middle name.

Quality Checks

While entering in all this metadata, it is very likely that somewhere along the way there will be human errors. Because of this it is important to check the metadata for these issues. You can also use data cleaning programs to find the patterns, missing values, character sets, and other characteristics of your data values.

PROVIDING ACCESS TO THE COLLECTIONS

How you choose to provide access to your digital collection depends on five major factors: functionality, familiarity, community, support, and cost.[7]

Functionality is very important in choosing a platform for your project because a platform that does not do what you need it to do will only complicate the project; you need a platform that will allow you to focus your time on preparing and entering your data, and not on learning how to navigate through the platform or figuring out workarounds for tasks that you need done but the platform does not seem to do. Depending on your type of data, you will find that some platforms work better than others. In other words, some platforms work very well with some types of data but less well with others. Ideally you will want to seek out an institution or organization that has worked with similar data and see what kind of platform they chose, and if they are happy with it. So, for example, if you are working on making an oral history collection available to the public, you would seek out others who have put together similar projects and reach out via email to ask them some questions about their chosen platform. Try to talk to at least two to three institutions, if possible.

Familiarity is another factor to look at, because choosing a platform that your users already have some familiarity with will lessen the learning curve required of your users.[8] Take a look at where your target users are currently getting their information from and see what platforms are being used to disseminate that information. The more familiar your potential users are with a platform, the more likely they are to use it. You will attract more users by using a platform they are already familiar with.

When deciding on a platform, look at the community who uses the platform to see if it is the right fit for your project.[9] In other words, if you are looking at a possible platform that is mostly used by a field that is in no way related to yours, that platform might not be suited to your needs. If the community is in your field or a related field, it will be easier for you to reach out to others when you have particular questions or are seeking advice.

Whatever platform you choose, it is very important you have support available to you. Support options include your IT department or Facebook groups or listservs catered to that particular platform. If the skills required for the platform are beyond your scope of knowledge, you may need more hands-on support, so be certain that you aren't in over your head. A less complicated platform may be a better choice.

Finally, we have to address cost. Before making a decision be sure to have an accurate estimate of the costs, including hosting fees, configuration costs, and ongoing maintenance fees.[10] If the platform you are interested in does not appear to be financially feasible, you may want to try to look at some free, open-source options. Some of the more popular free, open-source platforms include Omeka and Scalar. As suggested previously, do not be afraid to reach out to other institutions using these platforms and see how these options are working for them.

Marketing and Promotion

You now need to raise awareness with users and nonusers that your organization has lots of digital content available to access. You can raise awareness in the following ways:

- Start a blog. Blogs are fairly easy to create and allow you to grow an audience through regular posts.
- Use social media. If your organization has social media accounts, use these to spread the news about your project. Link to your blog on social media as well.
- Contact your local public radio and television stations. Reach out to these local stations to see if there is any interest in reporting on your project.
- Give lectures. If you are on a college or university campus, see if you can give a talk on your project.
- Collaborate. Find out if any organizations have a similar project or a complementary project. You may be able to work together to raise awareness.

PRESERVING THE COLLECTIONS

Preserving Analog Items

If your project's digital objects were not born digital, then you will need to make certain that the physical or analog items are also preserved. Digitizing items does not mean you can throw away the physical objects (unless they have deteriorated beyond a usable condition). However, it does mean that you can store the objects off-site and save your prime storage space for other objects in your collection.

Temperature

Control of temperature is important because heat accelerates deterioration. Deterioration is approximately doubled with each increase in temperature of 18 degrees Fahrenheit.[11] On the other side, temperatures that are too cold could cause embrittlement, hazing, and cracks in certain types of objects.[12] While there is no single temperature range that is ideal for all objects, a general guideline of a temperature between 65 and 68 degrees Fahrenheit is sufficient for most objects in your collection.

Relative Humidity

Next to temperature, regulating relative humidity is one of the most important factors in proper preservation of your materials. Having a high relative humidity "provides the moisture necessary to promote harmful chemical reactions in materials and, in combination with high temperature, encourages mold growth and insect activity."[13] Conversely, having an extremely low relative humidity "may lead to desiccation and embrittlement of some materials."[14] A general guideline recommends a relative humidity between 30 and 50 percent. It is also important that both your temperature and relative humidity remain stable and that fluctuations are kept to a minimum.

Storage

Your collections should be stored in appropriate archival folders and boxes on adequate shelving and in a storage area with appropriate temperature and relative humidity. If you find yourself with inadequate storage solutions and are limited financially from revamping your entire collection's storage, then start small. The ideal way to handle this situation is to replace the containers closest to the object first. This means first replace folders, then boxes, then shelving, then storage areas.

Handling

All objects must be handled with the utmost of care, as handling has a direct impact on the useful life of your collection. Here are some general guidelines to follow:

- Only clean hands or hands covered in white cotton gloves should handle objects.
- Use both hands when handling objects
- Keep work surfaces clean and uncluttered.

Preserving Digital Objects

Choosing Preservation File Formats

When you select file formats for your digital objects, you should consider the following criteria, recommended by the National Archives UK.

- Open Standards: It is recommended that the file format that you choose have its technical specifications available in the public domain. This is important because you will need access to detailed technical information about the file formats in which those records are preserved.[15]
- Ubiquity: It is recommended that the file format that you choose be a popular one. The advantage to choosing a popular format is that it will be supported by a wide range of software and will therefore tend to have broader and longer-lasting support from software suppliers, compared to those that only have a niche market.[16]
- Stability: It is recommended that the file format that you choose be stable and not subject to constant or major changes over time. In addition, any new versions of the format should also be backward compatible.[17]
- Metadata Support: It is recommended that the file format that you choose allow for the inclusion of metadata. An example of a format that includes metadata is a TIFF file. A TIFF file will most likely include metadata fields that will allow you to record details like the make and model of scanner, the software and operating system used, the name of the creator, and a description of the image.[18]
- Feature Set: It is recommended that the file format that you choose have a comprehensive range of features and functionality that satisfy your needs.
- Interoperability: It is recommended that the file format that you choose support interoperability.[19] In other words, your chosen file format should be able to share its metadata with external search engines, other users, and IT systems.
- Viability: It is recommended that the file format that you choose provide error-detection facilities to allow detection of file corruption.[20]

Create Multiple Copies

The greatest at-risk object in the world of digital preservation is the unique object. A unique object is a file that only exists on a single storage device, such as a thumb drive or floppy disk. The greatest strength of digital material is that you can easily make multiple copies of digital items. Below are three levels for preserving your digital items via creating multiple copies. The basic level is for small budgets with very little institutional technical support and infrastructure. The medium level is for medium-sized institutions/budgets with moderate support and infrastructure. The advanced level is for large institutions with major budgets and major infrastructure.

- Basic Level: Take your uncompressed digital files and put them on two different external hard drives.
- Medium Level: Basic-level copies PLUS copies on cloud storage.
- Advanced Level: Medium-level copies PLUS copies on an IT-controlled redundant server with regular backing up via tape drive.

Metadata

As mentioned in the previous chapter, preservation metadata provides the information needed to carry out the preservation and access of your digital resources. It also establishes the authenticity of digital content, and records the chain of custody and provenance for a digital resource.[21] Examples of preservation metadata include documentation of any actions that are taken to preserve your objects (such as data refreshing and migration) and of any changes occurring during digitization or preservation.[22] When you collect this data you will input it into a digital preservation system like Archivematica or Preservica.

Security

Securing your digital objects is also part of digital preservation. You must physically secure your items and also protect them from theft or viruses.

Physical Security

You need to know the physical location of your digital objects, and you also need to make certain that the physical location is protected. This means that you need to protect these objects from environmental conditions such as temperature and humidity.

Theft

You also need to protect these objects from theft by managing who has access to your network. Think about creating levels of access for the staff with password-encrypted files.

Viruses

You will need to make sure you have some sort of virus protection for your network and for incoming material.

CONCLUSION

In this chapter you have learned the basic steps to a digital curation project, how to digitize your chosen objects, how to accurately describe the objects and collection, how to provide access to your collection, and how to preserve your analog and digital objects. In the coming chapters we will move beyond these general steps and get more detailed, as we look at the most common digital curation projects libraries, archives, and museums undertake.

NOTES

1. "Objects Principle 1," National Information Standards Organization, last updated September 3, 2008, http://framework.niso.org/37.html.
2. "Objects Principle 3," National Information Standards Organization, last updated April 17, 2008, http://framework.niso.org/20.html.
3. "Objects Principle 5," National Information Standards Organization, last updated April 17, 2008, http://framework.niso.org/22.html.
4. "Objects Principle 6," National Information Standards Organization, last updated April 17, 2008, http://framework.niso.org/23.html.
5. Setting up Excel Spreadsheets for Single Item or Compound Object Metadata. March 6, 2012. https://nyheritage.org/sites/default/files/pages/MetadataExcel.pdf.
6. "Metadata," National Information Standards Organization, last updated April 17, 2008, http://framework.niso.org/24.html.
7. "Choosing a Platform for Your Project Website," Digital Humanities at Berkeley, accessed October 3, 2017, http://digitalhumanities.berkeley.edu/blog/13/12/04/choosing-platform-your-project-website.
8. "Choosing a Platform," Digital Humanities at Berkeley.
9. "Choosing a Platform," Digital Humanities at Berkeley.
10. "Choosing a Platform," Digital Humanities at Berkeley.
11. Sherelyn Ogden, "2.1 Temperature, Relative Humidity, Light, and Air Quality: Basic Guidelines for Preservation," Northeast Document Conservation Center, accessed April 7, 2017, https://www.nedcc.org/free-resources/preservation-leaflets/2.-the-environment/2.1-temperature,-relative-humidity,-light,-and-air-quality-basic-guidelines-for-preservation.
12. "Temperature and Relative Humidity (RH)," American Museum of Natural History, accessed April 4, 2017, http://www.amnh.org/our-research/natural-science-collections-conservation/general-conservation/preventive-conservation/temperature-and-relative-humidity-rh/.
13. "Temperature and Relative Humidity," American Museum of Natural History.
14. "Temperature and Relative Humidity," American Museum of Natural History.

15. Adrian Brown, "Digital Preservation Guidance Note 1: Selecting File Formats for Long-Term Preservation," issue 2, The National Archives (August 2008), https://www.nationalarchives.gov.uk/documents/selecting-file-formats.pdf.

16. Brown, "Selecting File Formats."
17. Brown, "Selecting File Formats."
18. Brown, "Selecting File Formats."
19. Brown, "Selecting File Formats."
20. Brown, "Selecting File Formats."
21. "Glossary," National Digital Stewardship Alliance, Digital Library Federation, accessed April 7, 2017, http://ndsa.org/glossary/.
22. Murtha Baca, ed., *Introduction to Metadata*, 3rd ed. (Los Angeles: Getty Research Institute, 2016).

Chapter Four

Photograph Collections

DIGITIZATION

Choosing What to Digitize

Use the rubric in the priority list from chapter 2 to determine which photographs you should include in your digital collection. Here is a quick recap of the selection criteria:

Value

Do the photographs have great historical value to your community and/or researchers? The greater the historical value, the higher it should be on the priority list.

Demand

Are the photographs in high demand? Do researchers regularly request this item? If there is little to no demand, then place this item low on your priority list.

Condition of Materials

Are the photographs already showing signs of deterioration, or are they in fairly good condition? You may want to prioritize photographs that are starting to show signs of deterioration. Decide if you will also prioritize photographs showing advanced signs of deterioration. A conservator will most likely have to work on these items before digitization, so you will need to take this added expense into account.

Legal and Ethical Issues

As part of your digital image project, your institution should establish a code of ethics associated with creation, manipulation, and distribution of these objects. The code of ethics should stipulate the way in which the files are generated and how those files are monitored, and state that no damage was done to the original objects in order to achieve the digital copy. Be certain to include language that clarifies acceptable and unacceptable manipulation. Be sure to state that no manipulation is allowed on master image files and that any unavoidable manipulation, such as cropping, is documented. As an added benefit, adhering to a code of ethics adds a layer of authenticity to the digital image files, so if, for instance, a researcher questions the authenticity or content of an image file, your code of ethics document can help relieve any doubts that a digital version of a collection object is real.[1]

It is also important to protect the integrity of your digital image collection, especially once posted on a website for public viewing. You may accomplish this goal in two ways. One is through watermarking the files; the other is copyright. Copyright notices come in many forms. They can apply to individual image files, groups of images, or entire websites.[2] See the Copyright and Intellectual Property Decisions Flowchart (figure 2.1) in chapter 2 for more information on this topic.

Availability

Are the photographs already available online? You should check if they are already online to avoid duplication. Check the Prints & Photographs Online Catalog of the Library of Congress for photos. ArchiveGrid may be another resource to check for already posted photos. Flickr might be yet another potentially useful resource. If the subject of the photographs is of a local nature, check on the websites of local historical societies for already posted photos.

Choosing Equipment

Hardware

Recommended hardware for photo digitization includes the following:

- PC or Mac. Make certain you have enough free space on your computer for this project. Space will vary depending on the size of your collection.
- Scanner. There are many options when it comes to choosing a scanner. The best way to make your decision when selecting a scanner is to make sure that the type of scanner is appropriate for your materials, that the

scanner has sufficient technical capabilities, and that the scanner fits within your budget.[3]

- Type

  - Form feed equipment is not acceptable for photographs.
  - Scanning equipment must feature controls to limit light and heat exposure to the items being scanned.
  - Scanning equipment must be properly sized to accommodate collection materials without causing damage.
  - Oversized photographs must be scanned using equipment that features a scanning bed that is as large or larger than the photo to be scanned.[4]

- Technical Capabilities

  - Bit Depth: To ensure that all relevant information is captured and for the most accurate capture of tonal values, you will want your image to be scanned at a higher bit depth and then scaled down (either internally or externally) to the desired bit depth.
  - Dynamic Range: The scanner you choose should meet or match the dynamic range of the photographs being digitized. This is particularly important for photos with lots of dark areas.[5]

- Budget

  - Consult with other institutions and organizations for their advice on scanners.
  - Compare the price of purchasing a scanner with outsourcing the digitization to a scanning service.[6]

- Color Reproduction

  - Choose a scanner that supports and accurately represents the color of your photographs.[7]

If you choose to digitally photograph your photos rather than scan them, you will need the following equipment:

- Digital Camera. A digital SLR camera is ideal. It should have a normal 50mm lens with no wide-angle distortion. It is recommended that you have your camera professionally cleaned to prevent dust specks from appearing in your images.

- Camera Tripod. Use this in conjunction with a cable release or remote shutter release. Maximizing stability is important to preserving maximum image quality. By using a cable release or remote shutter release, you remove any shift (and the resulting shift back) caused by pushing the camera.
- Lighting. Use two hot lights or clamp lights in conjunction with an umbrella or a hot light soft box to prevent shadows.
- Media Card Reader. You will need a card reader to transfer the images from the digital camera to your computer.
- Neutral Background. The background will allow you to take your photos without interference. It is recommended you use white or neutral gray seamless paper.[8]

For most of your photographs it will be easier and less complicated to use a scanner. However, there are times when you will want to use a digital camera instead. Some examples of photographs you may want to avoid scanning include:

- Very fragile photographs
- Photographs that are stuck firmly in an album; tearing them out may cause irreparable damage

Software

For this project you will need photo editing software such as:

- Adobe Photoshop
- Adobe Photoshop Lightroom
- Capture One
- PaintShop Pro
- DxO OpticsPro

Space Requirements

Physical Space

You will need a workspace that will accommodate all of your equipment. For the digitization of photographs, you will need:

- A work area for a computer and a scanner for capturing and editing your photos
- An area to hold all your physical photos
- An area to set up your camera, tripod, and lights, if you are choosing to digitize your photos with a digital camera instead of a scanner

Digital Storage Space

When you scan your photos you will be creating a preservation file and an access file. This means this project is going to require a great deal of storage space. The actual amount of gigabytes needed will vary depending on how large your photo collection is.

Digitization Workflow

In-House Digitization

If you have decided to complete the digitization in-house, use the In-House Workflow Chart for Photograph Collections (figure 4.1) as a guideline for your project.

Prepare the Photographs

Step 1: Inspect for damage. Check the photographs for signs of deterioration and/or damage.

Inspect for physical damage. Physical damage like rips or tears in your items will mean you will have to fix those items before they can be scanned. Photos damaged by mold will need to be isolated from the rest of the collection and a conservator may need to be consulted.

Inspect for chemical deterioration. Items to look out for include foxing (aging stains), adhesion of gelatin layers (from high humidity), and flaking emulsions (from low humidity).

Step 2: Clean photographs. Use a soft brush or a dust blower, like those used to clean a camera lens, to remove dust from each photo before you scan it.

Step 3: Restore photos. Make certain that all photographs that need restoration are sent to a conservator and restoration is complete before scanning.

Prepare the Equipment (if using a scanner)

Step 1: Clean the scanner. Use glass cleaner to clean your scanner by spraying the glass cleaner on a lint-free towel and using it to wipe the glass.

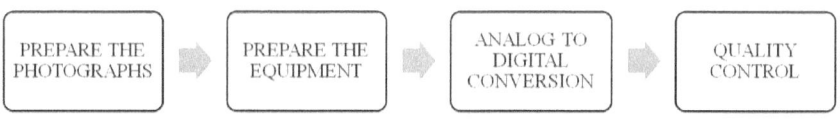

Figure 4.1. In-House Workflow Chart for Photograph Collections

If you have any glass parts that are prone to fingerprints, make sure that they are cleaned before each use.

Step 2: Regularly maintain the scanner. Clean the scanner on a weekly basis when in use.

Prepare the Equipment (if using a digital camera)

Step 1: Place photograph flat on a table.

Step 2: Set up the digital camera. The camera should ideally be on a tripod for stability.

Step 3: Set up lighting. Use two strobe lights with lighting umbrellas, positioned so that they even out the light source.

Step 4: Take photo. Make sure that you have the desired focus, exposure, and composition.

Analog to Digital Conversion

Using the guidelines from the Federal Agencies Digital Guidelines Initiative (FADGI), the master file format for your digital objects should be in either TIFF, JPEG 2000, or PDF/A format. The recommended resolution rate should be set between 100 pixels per inch (ppi) and 600 ppi (100 ppi being the lowest acceptable rate.) The recommended bit depth rate should be between 8 and 16 (8 being the lowest acceptable rate.) The recommended color space to use is either Adobe RGB (1998) ProPhoto, or eciRGB_v2. Grey Gamma 2.2 and sRGB are also accepted but only receive 1 star on FADGI's scale of 1–4 stars (4 being the best). FADGI also recommends that these digital objects are in color.[9] Grayscale is also accepted, but it only receives 1 star on FADGI's scale of 1–4 stars.

From your master file, you will create an access file. FADGI guidelines state that no image retouching of master files will be permitted. You may wish to make a copy of your master TIFF file, retouch that image, and then create a smaller JPEG file for access. Finally, you will save all your files. Keep the original unedited files in a master files folder. Keep edited files and JPEG files in an access folder.

Quality Control

Make certain that all digital images created are satisfactory. If they are not, you must attempt to digitize them again. If you are working with a large collection of images, it is acceptable to spot-check digital images by a certain number of intervals for quality. (For example, you can spot-check every twentieth recording for quality control. Also check that your image files are named correctly. *See the* File Naming *section in this chapter for more information.*

Outsourcing Digitization

If your organization is choosing to outsource your digitization, you should follow the Outsourcing Digitization Workflow Chart for Photograph Collections (figure 4.2) as a guideline.

1. Document the photographs being outsourced. Make a list of all the photographs that you are sending out for digitization.
2. Inspect the photographs before sending. List the condition of each object.
3. Properly pack the photographs. Create a set of instructions on how to properly pack your photographs, and make sure staff follow the instructions.
4. Document the shipment and sign a loan form. Somewhere in your project notes you should list the date that your photographs were shipped to the outside vendor, and you should make sure you have a copy of a signed loan form.
5. Perform quality control of the finished project. Check the digital files received and make sure they are to your satisfaction. Also make sure that you check the list you created in step 1 so that you can confirm that all the photographs sent out were returned and that they are still in the same condition as when they left your possession.

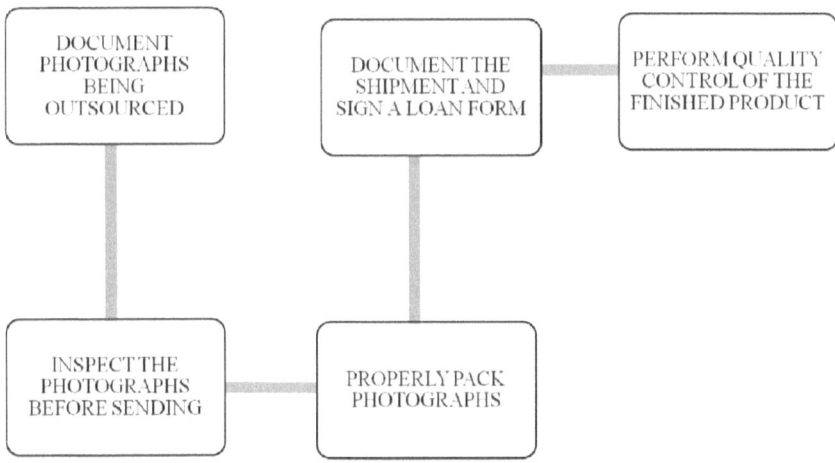

Figure 4.2. Outsourcing Digitization Workflow Chart for Photograph Collections

Chapter 4
DESCRIBING THE COLLECTION

File Naming

When naming photo files, a basic file name might include the date of the image, one or more subject type descriptors, and a number to indicate the version of the photo.

As an example, you may have a collection of images from the city of Paris. The first image is of the Eiffel Tower, and it was taken on November 3, 2007.

- The date would appear as: 20071103
- The location of the image: Paris
- The subject of image: Eiffel Tower
- The version of the photo (most likely three digits is enough, but you might need more, depending on your collection): 001, 002, etc.
- The file type extension: .jpg or .tiff
- The file name of this image would be 20071103_paris_eiffeltower_001.tiff
- Other file names from the collection might be

  - 20071103_paris_eiffeltower_002.tiff (a second photo of the Eiffel Tower)
  - 20071103_paris_sacrecoeur_001.tiff (a photo of Sacre Coeur)
  - 20071103_paris_notredame_003.tiff (a third photo of Notre Dame)

If your photographs have accession numbers, you will most likely want to add these numbers to the file name.

Metadata

For image collections, most organizations use VRA Core or Dublin Core for their metadata needs. Whichever metadata schema you decide on using, the information you are looking to capture can be found by answering these questions:

- Who is involved with this image? (Who took it, who owns it, who is in it?)
- What is interesting about this image?
- Where is this image from?
- When was this image created or modified?

Some institutions prefer to embed as much descriptive metadata as possible into digital images, so that the metadata can move along with the image and so that digital images can be searched easily, while others use a spreadsheet to organize their metadata. It is also possible to do both; you can supplement the embedded metadata with a spreadsheet.

If you plan to add your spreadsheet to a content management system you will most likely have to make sure that the spreadsheet contains only the metadata fields that your content management system accepts.

PROVIDING ACCESS

Choosing a Platform

Now that your photos are digital, you will need to make sure that your users have access to these files. You will need to choose a content management system or digital asset management system that works best for your collection. Some organizations with digital photograph collections choose to use the following systems:

- Omeka: A free, open-source content management system for online digital collections
- CollectionSpace: A free, open-source collections management application that meets the needs of museums, historical societies, biological collections, and other collections-holding organizations
- CONTENTdm: A digital asset management system run by OCLC; can be costly for institutions on a small budget

Organizations that have a small budget, but do not have the technical skills to work with Omeka or CollectionSpace, may want to consider using Flickr for their image collections.

Promotion and Marketing

Let's take a look at how various organizations market and promote their digital image collections.

The University of Iowa Libraries use social media to promote their collections in many different ways. They strive to share with users the breadth and variety of their special collections. The University of Iowa Libraries Special Collections department posts photographs of items in their digital collection on Instagram.

The British Library uses Flickr, a website for hosting images, to post many photos from their digital image collection. The posting of images on Flickr allows the library to gain a wider audience than if the images were only located on the British Library's website.

Cornell University has an initiative in which information about their image collections can be entered into Wikipedia and searched; this creates a wider user base for their images.

Other ideas for promoting your digital image collection include the following:

- Create a weekly Facebook photo album to show off your newest content.
- Tweet out links to your newest digital images and use relevant hashtags to promote them.
- Put a link to your digital collection at the most visible spot on your organization's home page.

PRESERVATION

Preserving Analog Items

Temperature

The International Organization for Standardization recommends a temperature range for photographs from 35 to 65 degrees Fahrenheit, depending on the type of photograph and the length of storage (ten years; indefinitely). (See ISO 18920, "Imaging Materials—Reflection Prints—Storage Practices," 2011.)

Relative Humidity

The relative humidity in a storage area containing black and white photographs should be between 30 percent and 50 percent. The recommended relative humidity for color photographs is between 20 percent and 50 percent.

Storage

There are a variety of options for storing your photographs. Plastic sleeves are a good storage enclosure option because of their transparency; they allow you to view photos without removing them from the enclosures. If you choose to use plastic enclosures, make sure they are made of either polyethylene, polypropylene, or polyester. Polyvinyl chloride is not an acceptable plastic.

Paper sleeves are another good storage enclosure option. Make certain that the paper sleeves or envelopes are lignin free and that they have passed the Photographic Activity Test (PAT).

Handling

When handling your photographs, it is recommended that you use nitrile gloves. Latex gloves are usually not recommended because many people are allergic to latex. Many organizations use cotton gloves, which are an acceptable option if you do not have nitrile gloves handy, but beware of potential issues with cotton gloves. They can be bulky, and it can be quite difficult to truly remove all the dust from cotton gloves.

Preserving Digital Objects

Your digital photos should ideally be in JPEG (for access) and TIFF, JPEG 2000, or PDF/A file formats (for preservation). The JPEG file is smaller than a TIFF, JPEG 2000, or PDF/A file and is perfectly suitable for your organization's users to view. Your preservation or master file will be much larger than the JPEG file but will be accessed much less regularly; it will be your preservation file. If you should ever need to produce another JPEG file, you will create it through your master file. Remember to monitor and recopy data as necessary, and to outline a migration strategy for transferring your digital images and associated metadata to future formats. For further information on digital preservation, see the guidelines in the section titled "Preserving Digital Objects" in chapter 3.

CONCLUSION

In this chapter you learned how to create and curate a digital photograph collection. You can decide which items to digitize using the priority list, and you can properly digitize your images using either the in-house or outsourcing digitization workflow charts. You are aware of the legal and ethical issues surrounding digitizing images and the importance of protecting the integrity of your digital image collection. In addition, you now know what type of metadata to capture for your project, and you have been given some examples of access platforms and promotion and marketing techniques of other organizations to make sure your project is recognized by researchers for its immense value. Furthermore, you have guidelines on best practices for preserving both your analog and digital objects. To close this chapter, you have been provided with a Digital Image Project Checklist (table 4.1) that will help you through your project.

Table 4.1. Digital Image Project Checklist

Steps	Checklist	Notes
Choosing What to Digitize	Have you used the priority rubric to create a priority list of recordings to digitize?	
Preparation of Recordings	Are any conservation techniques needed for your recordings?	
Preparation of Equipment	Have you checked all of your hardware and software settings to prepare for the conversion?	
Analog to Digital Conversion	Are your digital objects created in accordance with listed guidelines? Preservation Format: AIFF, BWF, WAV Sampling Rate: 96 kHz Bit Depth: 24	
File Creation	Have you created a preservation file for each recording?	
	Have you created an access file for each recording?	
File Naming	Have you chosen a file-naming convention and checked its consistency across all project files?	
Metadata	Have you created and checked the metadata for your preservation files?	
	Have you created and checked the metadata for your access files?	
Access	Have you chosen an access platform for your digital project?	
	Have you generated promotion and marketing ideas for your digital project?	
Preservation	Are physical objects preserved according to best practices?	
	Have you performed a checksum for your preservation file folder?	
	Have you performed a checksum for your access file folder?	
Storage	Have you saved your preservation files to storage?	

Steps	Checklist	Notes
	Have you saved your access files to storage?	

NOTES

1. J. M. Koelling, *Digital Imaging: A Practical Approach* (Lanham, MD: Rowman & Littlefield, 2004).

2. Koelling, *Digital Imaging*.

3. Kit A. Peterson, "What to Look for in a Scanner: Tip Sheet for Digitizing Pictorial Materials in Cultural Institutions," Prints & Photographs Division, Library of Congress, June 2005, https://www.loc.gov/rr/print/tp/LookForAScanner.pdf.

4. "Collections Care," Library of Congress, accessed May 15, 2017, https://www.loc.gov/preservation/care/scan.html.

5. Peterson, "What to Look for in a Scanner."

6. Peterson, "What to Look for in a Scanner."

7. Peterson, "What to Look for in a Scanner."

8. "Tips and Tools for Digitizing a Museum Collection," ONLINE Magazine, http://www.infotoday.com/online/nov11/Avila-Sanders-Martin-Tips-and-Tools-for-Digitizing-a-Museum-Collection.shtml.

9. "Federal Agency Digital Guidelines Initiative," accessed October 13, 2017, http://www.digitizationguidelines.gov/.

Chapter Five

Newspaper Collections

DIGITIZATION

Choosing What to Digitize

Because newspapers are highly acidic and have a fast rate of deterioration, many organizations that have large newspaper collections are choosing to digitize them. Use the priority list in chapter 3 to determine which newspapers you should include in your digital collection. Here's a quick recap of things to consider when assigning priority:

Value

Does the newspaper have great historical value to your community and/or researchers? The greater the historical value, the higher it should be on the priority list.

Demand

Is this newspaper in high demand? Do researchers regularly request this item? If there is little to no demand, then place this item low on your priority list.

Condition of Materials

Is the newspaper already showing signs of deterioration or is it in fairly good condition? Normally you may want to start with the items in the best condition because they will have a relatively easy and smooth digitization process; items in need of conservation will hold up your project. On the other hand, due to the high deterioration rate of newspapers, you may want to put very fragile but still readable items high on your priority list.

Legal and Ethical Issues

Is this newspaper under copyright protection? Newspapers that can be digitized include any newspapers published in the United States before 1923. Newspapers published before 1923 are in the public domain, even if they have the © copyright symbol; therefore, you can digitize and provide access to these without any concern over copyright. You can also digitize any newspapers published between 1923 and 1977 without a copyright notice. Newspapers published before 1978 without the © copyright symbol are in the public domain. If the newspapers in question have copyright protection, you can only digitize them if you have the permission of the copyright owner or if your use falls into the category of permitted uses, called "fair use."[1]

Availability

Is this newspaper already available online? Items that have been digitized by another organization will be low on the priority list. If you want to see if your newspaper has already been digitized, a good place to start is the Chronicling America collection, a collection of historic American newspapers published between 1836 and 1922, at the Library of Congress's website.

Choosing Equipment

Hardware

Recommended hardware for a newspaper digitization project includes the following:

- PC or Mac. Make certain you have enough free space on your computer for this project. Space will vary depending on the size of your collection.
- Scanner or Digital Camera. If you have fragile items, you are going to want to use a digital camera; otherwise a scanner will work for most projects, just make sure it can accommodate the size of your newspapers. For more information on choosing a scanner or digital camera, see chapter 4.
- Film scanner. Your newspapers might have already been put on microfilm, since it is the accepted standard for preserving newspapers. If this is the case, you will need a film scanner in order to digitize your materials. If it is not, you may want to consider having your newspapers microfilmed before being digitized. Otherwise, you can still digitize newspapers from print copy.

Software

Whether you choose to use a scanner or a digital camera, you will need image editing software to edit each object. The most popular image editing software still remains Adobe Photoshop; however, if you are looking for a low-cost/no-cost option, GIMP is a free open-source software that will allow you to edit your TIFF files.

Space Requirements

Physical Space

You will need a workspace that will accommodate all your equipment. For the digitization of newspapers, you will need:

- a work area for a computer
- an area to hold all your newspapers
- a work area for a flatbed scanner, should you decide to use a scanner
- an area to set up your camera, tripod, and lights, should you decide to use a digital camera

Digital Storage Space

TIFF files are normally quite large, and are even larger when combined with the large dimensions of a newspaper, so be prepared to have a lot of digital space for this project. To give you an idea of how much space you will need, an 8x10 image scanned at 600 ppi will produce a TIFF that is approximately 84.4 MB.[2]

Digitization Workflow

In-House

If you have decided to complete the digitization in-house, use the In-House Workflow Chart for Newspaper Collections (figure 5.1) as a guideline for your project.

Prepare the Newspapers

Step 1: Bound newspapers will inhibit optical character recognition accuracy, so if your newspapers are bound you will need to unbind them for this project.

    Step 2: Any folded or creased pages will need to be unfolded and flattened, and tears will need to be mended. Consult a conservator for complex problems.

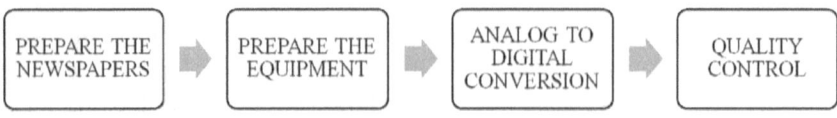

Figure 5.1.   In-House Workflow Chart for Newspaper Collections

How to unbind a newspaper:

1. Remove cover boards and end sheets
2. Remove glue and sewing from text block
3. Trim glue and thread from inner margins of pages [3]

How to unfold and flatten a newspaper:

1. Sweep newspaper with a soft, natural fiber brush.
2. Place plastic sheeting on a table.
3. Cover plastic sheeting with a layer of wet blotters.
4. Cover wet blotters with spun polyester.
5. Place newspapers down.
6. Lightly mist papers with water.
7. Tent the entire table with plastic sheeting and secure around the edges with weights.
8. Wait 4 hours.
9. Take 6–10 pages at a time and place them in a stack, as demonstrated in figure 5.2.

This stack should be placed under weights or secured in a book press at least overnight (preferably 24 hours) to get the maximum benefit from the humidification process. [4]

If the newspaper is not flattened to your satisfaction, you can repeat the process up to three times, but make sure that the newspapers are allowed to dry thoroughly between each session. Newspapers that have not been adequately flattened after three attempts should be treated by a conservator. [5]

Repairing Tears

Repairing tears in the pages of a newspaper should only be performed as needed to allow the material to be handled during preparation and digitization.

1. Place a piece of binding board under the area being repaired to prevent breakage of pages.

Figure 5.2. How to Unfold and Flatten a Newspaper

2. Apply archival mending tape.
3. Apply tape firmly and smooth it out with a bone folder.[6]

Prepare the Equipment (if using a scanner)

Step 1: Clean the scanner. Use glass cleaner to clean your scanner. Spray the glass cleaner on a lint-free towel and then use it to wipe the glass. If you have any glass parts that are prone to fingerprints, make sure that they are cleaned before each use.

Step 2: Regularly maintain the scanner. Clean the scanner on a weekly basis when in use.

Prepare the Equipment (if using a digital camera)

Step 1: Place photograph flat on a table.
Step 2: Set up the digital camera. The camera should ideally be on a tripod for stability.
Step 3: Set up lighting. Use two strobe lights with lighting umbrellas, positioned so that they even out the light source.
Step 4: Take photo. Make sure that you have the desired focus, exposure, and composition to properly capture your newspaper page.

Analog to Digital Conversion

Using the guidelines from the Federal Agencies Digital Guidelines Initiative (FADGI), the master file format for your digital objects should be either TIFF, JPEG 2000, or PDF/A. The recommended resolution rate should be set between 150 ppi and 400 ppi (100 ppi being the lowest acceptable rate). The recommended bit depth should be 8. The recommended color space to use is either Grey Gamma 2.2 or sRGB. FADGI also recommends that these digital images be in color.[7] Greyscale is also acceptable, though not as desirable.

From your master file, you will create an access file. FADGI guidelines state that no image retouching of master files will be permitted. You may wish to make a copy of your master TIFF, JPEG 2000, or PDF/A file, retouch that image, and then create a smaller JPG file for access. If you need to edit your image, follow these steps:

1. Clean up the image in a photo editor (remove dirt, reduce noise, etc.).
2. Crop page images to the page edge.
3. De-skew any pages exhibiting more than 3 degrees of skew.
4. Split double page frames (newspapers filmed two sheets per frame) into a single page image (one image per page).
5. If the newspaper is printed in black and white, use 8-bit grayscale.
6. If the newspaper is printed with all or some pages in color, use 24-bit color.
7. From this edited file, create a JPG file for access.[8]

Finally, you will save all your files. Keep the original unedited files in a master files folder. Keep edited files and JPEG files in an access folder.

Quality Control

Make certain that all digital images created are satisfactory. If they are not, you must attempt to digitize them again. If you are working with a large collection of images, it is acceptable to spot-check digital images by a certain number of intervals for quality (example: spot-check every Nth image for quality control). Also check that your image files are named correctly. *See* File Naming *section in this chapter for more information.*

Outsourcing Digitization

If your collection is small, it may be more cost effective to outsource the digitization than to do it in-house. Usually with rather large collections outsourcing can get expensive, but you may still choose to outsource if you simply do not have enough staff on hand to digitize the collection. Another reason you might choose to outsource your digitization is if you are working within a short time frame; a digitization service will probably be able to get your newspapers digitized faster than you can. When you choose a service provider, make sure to tell them if you will be requesting that actual newspapers be digitized or that microfilm of the newspapers be digitized. Make sure the vendor has experience with whichever format you will be sending them.

Once you have chosen a vendor, consult the Outsourcing Digitization Workflow Chart for Newspaper Collections (figure 5.3) for guidance.

1. Document the newspapers being outsourced. Make a list of all the newspapers that you are sending out for digitization.
2. Inspect the newspapers before sending. List the condition of each object.
3. Properly pack the newspapers. Create a set of instructions on how to properly pack your newspapers, and make sure staff follow the instructions.
4. Document the shipment and sign a loan form. Somewhere in your project notes you should list the date that your newspapers were shipped to the outside vendor, and you should make sure you have a copy of a signed loan form.
5. Perform quality control of the finished project. Check the digital files received and make sure they are to your satisfaction. Also make sure that you check the list you created in step 1 so that you can confirm all the newspapers that were sent out were returned and that they are still in the same condition as when they left your possession.

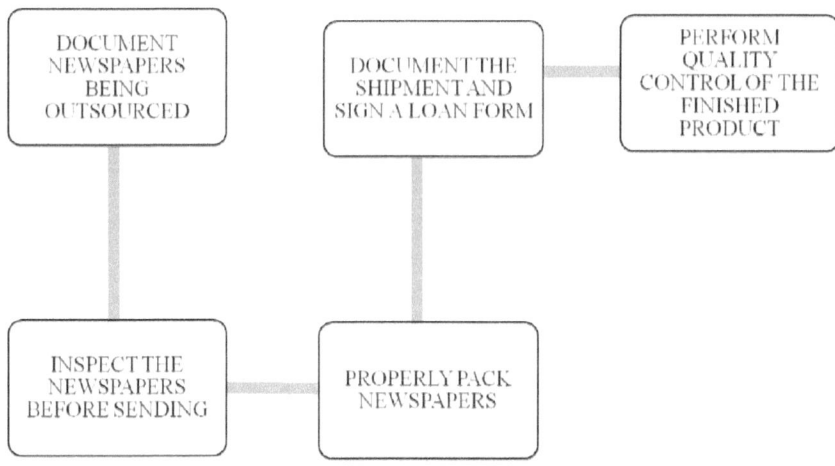

Figure 5.3. Outsourcing Digitization Workflow Chart for Newspaper Collections

DESCRIBING THE COLLECTION

File Naming

Each of your newspaper issues should have a separate folder. Each folder should follow the same naming convention. Ideally it will have a naming convention that includes an abbreviation of the newspaper's title, year, volume number, issue number, and date:

- Title: XXX
- Year: XXXX
- Volume Number: XXX
- Issue Number: XXX
- Date: MMDDYYYY

For each item in the folder you will want to add the same information as above, plus the page number:

- Page Number: XXX

Let's look at an example for clarification. You have a scan from a *Springfield Morning News* newspaper from October 27, 1954. It is volume number 20 and issue number 43. Your scan is of page 55. You would name this file SMN_1954_20_43_10271954_55. The folder this file would go into would be SMN_1954_20_43_10271954.

If you are using particular software, like Olive Software for example, it will most likely have its own file-naming conventions.

Another file naming option would be to use the Library of Congress Catalog Number (LCCN) for each title, followed by the issue date (YYYYMMDD) and page number. You can find the right LCCN in the catalog record of the *US Newspaper Directory, 1690–Present* at the Library of Congress website. Be aware that sometimes the Sunday paper has a different title. If this is noted on the record for the daily title, use the LCCN for the daily.[9]

OCR and Metadata

After your digital images have been created they will need to be processed with optical character recognition software, which scans your image files, recognizes the printed text within the images, and converts that text into machine-readable digital text documents. This text can then be added as metadata to a digital archive, either on collections management software or a website, and associated with the image it was scanned from to allow keyword searching of the text content.[10] Most OCR software will let you save this text in whatever format is convenient for you (.doc, .pdf, .txt, .rtf, etc.).

When it comes to the most common types of metadata used in newspaper digitization projects, you will most likely find yourself using ALTO and METS. According to the Library of Congress, Analyzed Layout and Text Object (ALTO) is an XML Schema that details technical metadata for describing the layout and content of physical text resources, such as pages of a book or a newspaper. ALTO most commonly serves as an extension schema used within the Metadata Encoding and Transmission Schema (METS) administrative metadata section, and the combination of METS and ALTO is the current industry standard for newspaper digitization used by hundreds of modern, large-scale newspaper digitization projects.[11] However, ALTO instances can also exist as stand-alone documents used independently of METS.[12]

PROVIDING ACCESS

Choosing a Platform

There are a variety of options when it comes to choosing a platform to host your digitized newspapers. The Cambridge Public Library chose to use Veridian to host its digital collection of historic Cambridge newspapers. The reasons for choosing Veridian include its ease of use and quick search turnaround time, as well as "its ability to overcome the technical challenges of delivering historical, digitized newspapers online by preserving the original newspaper layout."[13] Veridian also allows users to fix textual errors created during the digitization process, which helps to enhance search results for everyone.[14] The Vassar College Libraries also chose Veridian for its sophisticated search engine and the ability to instantly share articles via social media.[15]

Olive Software's ActivePaper Archive is another popular software platform. It is used by the Brooklyn Public Library, Penn State, and the Colorado State Library.[16]

Marketing and Promotion

Let's take a look at some ways to market and promote your digital newspaper collection.

1. Harness the Press.
   The Ulukau Hawaiian Electronic Library has a digital newspaper archive known as the Hoʻolaupaʻi Hawaiian Nūpepa Collection,

which contains Hawaiian-language newspapers. The site was officially released to the media during the annual Native Hawaii Education Convention. Timing the collection's release to coincide with the convention allowed for a bigger audience and led to an article on the front page of the local newspaper, which led to a radio station picking up the story, which led to TV stations picking up the story for their evening news programs. The publicity for their collection allowed the library to reach so many interested educators and members of the community.

2. Social Media.

The Vassar College Libraries had a collection of nineteenth- and twentieth-century student newspapers, and in 2011 they began digitizing this collection. Part of their marketing strategy included creating a blog, a Facebook page, and a Twitter account. Once a month, the college archivist began posting links to newspaper articles featuring news events that occurred on that particular day in history.[17]

This strategy of social media marketing provided a new opportunity for the libraries to link to their newspaper content and reach an audience of both current and former students, as well as other interested parties.[18]

3. Surveys.

The California Digital Newspaper Collection conducted surveys of its users and found that users tended to be older, so they geared their marketing toward more "traditional forms of communication like emails and posting to listservs."[19] An added benefit to conducting surveys regularly is that you can see if your current demographic changes and modify your marketing for that new demographic.

PRESERVATION

Preserving Analog Items

Temperature

The Library of Congress (LOC) recommends that newspapers be stored at room temperature or below. The Northeast Documentation Conservation Center (NEDCC) recommends a stable temperature that is no higher than 70 degrees Fahrenheit for paper-based materials. You'll want to avoid high temperatures because heat will speed up the chemical deterioration of your newspapers.

Relative Humidity

The LOC recommends a relatively dry environment for newspapers and suggests a relative humidity of 35 percent. The NEDCC recommends a stable relative humidity between a minimum of 30 percent and a maximum of 50 percent. Keep in mind that a relative humidity above 70 percent will almost guarantee mold growth, so a high relative humidity should be avoided at all costs.

Storage

If your newspapers have not yet turned yellow, you may want to consider spraying them with deacidification spray to safely and effectively neutralize acid in the paper. The most popular spray is known as Bookkeeper. The 5.29 oz. bottle will treat roughly 16.5 square feet of paper, and the 32 oz. refills treat 100 square feet. If you have a rather large collection this can be costly, so take your budget into consideration before taking on this task. As a point of note, this product can only prevent your newspapers from yellowing; if they are already yellow then discoloration cannot be reversed, though the spray can possibly mitigate further yellowing.

Make sure to store your newspapers flat in acid-free, buffered folders that will be placed inside acid-free, buffered storage boxes. The alkaline buffer will help neutralize any acids that might migrate from your newspapers.

Handling

When handling newspapers, follow these guidelines put forth by the Library of Congress:

- Have clean hands and a clean, large work table on which to put the newspaper.
- Keep the newspaper flat and fully supported on the table during use.
- Keep food and drink away.
- Never fold the paper back on itself.
- Refold the paper using the original center fold and neatly align the edges.
- Do not use paper clips, "dog ear" folding, acidic inserts, rubber bands, self-adhesive tape, and/or glue on newspapers and clippings.[20]

Preserving Digital Objects

You will have both image files and optical character recognition (OCR) text files to preserve for this project. Based on FADGI recommendations, your master image files should be saved in TIFF, JPEG 2000, or PDF/A format for digital preservation, and your access files will most likely be saved as JPEG files. The National Library of Australia recommends converting text documents to Rich Text Format (RTF) for preservation. The Smithsonian Institution Archives recommends converting files to PDF/A, PDF, or RTF format. Choose a format that works best for your institution and your project. For further details on digital preservation, see the guidelines in the section on Preserving Digital Objects (chapter 3) for further details on digital preservation.

CONCLUSION

In this chapter you learned how to create and curate a digital newspaper collection. Using the priority list, you can create a list of which newspapers to digitize and using either the in-house or outsourcing digitization workflow charts you can properly digitize those newspapers. You are aware of the legal and ethical issues surrounding digitizing newspapers that were produced in the United States. In addition, you learned about Optical Character Recognition and its role in your project. You know what type of metadata to capture for your project and that METS and ALTO are the current industry standards for newspaper digitization. Lastly, you have been provided with a Digital Newspaper Project Checklist (table 5.1) to help you through your project.

Table 5.1. Digital Newspaper Project Checklist

Steps	Checklist	Notes
Choosing What to Digitize	Have you used the priority rubric to create a priority list of newspapers to digitize?	
Preparation of Newspapers	Are any conservation techniques needed for your newspapers?	
Preparation of Equipment	Have you checked all of your hardware and software settings to prepare for the conversion?	
Analog to Digital Conversion	Are your digital objects created in accordance with listed guidelines? Preservation File Format: TIFF, JPEG 2000, PDF/A Resolution Rate: 100–600ppi File Bit Depth: 8–16 Color Space: Adobe RGB (1998), ProPhoto, eciRGB_v2 (FADGI rating: 4 stars) Color Space: Grey Gamma 2.2, sRGB (FADGI rating: 1 star)	
File Creation	Have you created a preservation file for each newspaper?	

Steps	Checklist	Notes
	Have you created an access file for each newspaper?	
File Naming	Have you chosen a file-naming convention, and are you ensuring its consistency across all project files?	
Metadata	Have you created and checked the metadata for your preservation files?	
	Have you created and checked the metadata for your access files?	
Access	Have you chosen an access platform for your digital project?	
	Have you generated promotion and marketing ideas for your digital project?	
Preservation	Are physical objects properly preserved according to best practices?	
	Have you performed a checksum for your preservation file folder?	
	Have you performed a checksum for your access file folder?	
Storage	Have you saved your preservation files to storage?	
	Have you saved your access files to storage?	

NOTES

1. Judy G. Russell, "Copyright and the Newspaper Article," The Legal Genealogist, March 19, 2012, http://www.legalgenealogist.com/2012/03/19/copyright-the-newspaper-article/.

2. "JPEG vs. TIFF for Scanning Photos, Slides, and Negatives," Digital Memories, accessed September 24, 2017, http://www.digitalmemoriesonline.net/scan/output/jpeg_vs_tiff.htm.

3. "USNP Preservation Microfilming Guidelines," Newspaper and Current Periodical Reading Room, Serial and Government Publications Division, Library of Congress, accessed October 4, 2017, http://www.loc.gov/rr/news/usnp/usnpprepp.html.

4. "USNP Preservation Microfilming Guidelines," Newspaper and Current Periodical Reading Room, Serial and Government Publications Division, Library of Congress, accessed October 4, 2017, http://www.loc.gov/rr/news/usnp/usnpprepp.html.

5. "How to Flatten Folded or Rolled Paper Documents," Society of Rocky Mountain Archivists, accessed October 4, 2017, http://www.srmarchivists.org/resources/preservation/preservation-publications/how-to-flatten-folded-or-rolled-paper-documents/.

6. "USNP Preservation Microfilming Guidelines," Newspaper and Current Periodical Reading Room, Serial and Government Publications Division, Library of Congress, accessed October 4, 2017, http://www.loc.gov/rr/news/usnp/usnpprepp.html.

7. "Federal Agency Digital Guidelines Initiative," http://www.digitizationguidelines.gov/.

8. "4.0 Best Practices for Newspaper Preservation," University Library, University of Illinois at Urbana-Champaign, last modified December 15, 2010, http://cms.library.illinois.edu/export/dcc/bestpractices/chapter_04_newspaperdigitization.html.

9. "Specifications for Digitizing the Newspapers of Connecticut," Connecticut State Library, accessed October 4, 2017, https://ctstatelibrary.org/newspaper_specs.

10. "Optical Character Recognition (OCR) Scanning," TownsWeb Archiving, accessed October 4, 2017, https://www.townswebarchiving.com/ocr-scanning-service/.

11. Stefan Boddie, "What is METS/ALTO?" Veridian, July 19, 2014, https://www.veridiansoftware.com/knowledge-base/metsalto/.

12. "ALTO: Technical Metadata for Layout and Text Objects," Standards, Library of Congress, accessed October 4, 2017, http://www.loc.gov/standards/alto/.

13. Frederick Zarndt et al. "Digital Collections: If You Build Them, Will They Visit?" (paper, IFLA WLIC, Singapore, 2013).

14. Zarndt et al. "Digital Collections."

15. Zarndt et al. "Digital Collections."

16. "Newspaper Digitization," History Philosophy and Newspaper Library, University of Illinois at Urbana-Champaign, accessed October 4, 2017, https://www.library.illinois.edu/hpnl/about/digitization/.

17. Frederick Zarndt et al. "Digital Collections: If You Build Them, Will They Visit?" (paper, IFLA WLIC, Singapore).

18. Zarndt et al. "Digital Collections."

19. Zarndt et al. "Digital Collections."

20. "Preservation Measures for Newspapers," Library of Congress, http://www.loc.gov/preservation/care/newspap.html.

Chapter Six

Rare Books

DIGITIZATION

Choosing What to Digitize

Value

Is your rare book or manuscript particularly valuable? Digitizing this object might protect it from theft. Rare books and manuscripts are common targets for thieves, and by digitizing these materials you have helped keep them out of harm's way. The British Library began digitizing maps in rare books when they discovered multiple thefts of these valuable maps had occurred.[1]

Demand

Is the rare book or manuscript in high demand? Do researchers regularly request this item? If the item is in high demand it should be high on your priority list.

Condition of Materials

Is the rare book or manuscript already showing signs of deterioration, or is it in fairly good condition? You may want to prioritize items that are starting to show beginning signs of deterioration. Decide if you will also prioritize materials showing advanced signs of deterioration. A conservator will most likely have to work on these items before digitization, so you will need to take this added expense into account.

Legal and Ethical Issues

Your rare books and manuscripts collection most likely contains objects that were published before 1923, which means they are in the public domain and no permission is needed to digitize them. If your materials were published in 1923 or later, you will need to see if the items were published with a © copyright symbol. Any rare books that were published between 1923 and 1977 without a copyright notice are also in the public domain. If they were published with a copyright notice, then they have copyright protection. This means you can only digitize these objects if you have the permission of the copyright owner or if your use falls into a category of permitted uses, called "fair use."[2]

Availability

The following resources can help you determine if the materials you wish to digitize are already available in a digital format.

- Early American Fiction Collection (http://www.proquest.com/products-services/early_am_fiction.html)
- Early English Books Online (https://eebo.chadwyck.com/home)
- Early European Books (http://www.proquest.com/products-services/databases/eeb.html)
- Eighteenth Century Collections Online (https://quod.lib.umich.edu/e/ecco/)
- Making of America (https://quod.lib.umich.edu/m/moagrp/)
- Rare Book Room (http://www.rarebookroom.org/)

Choosing Equipment

Hardware

You need to be particular about the type of scanner you choose for digitizing rare books and manuscripts; a scanner used for mass digitization projects will most likely not cut it, due to the generally fragile nature of rare books and manuscripts. Ideally, you should use manually operated planetary book scanners without glass or plastic platens.[3] However, if you have medieval manuscripts or any other materials that have minute details, the International Federation of Library Associations and Institutions (IFLA) recommends digitizing with a high-resolution digital camera. They also recommend that, whichever method you choose, you use that method to digitize the entire project, in order to provide uniformity.[4] You will also need a PC or Mac that has sufficient storage space.

Software

You will need photo editing software for this project. Adobe Photoshop is a popular software, and so is GIMP, an open-source, free software that will allow you to edit your image files.

Space Requirements

Physical Space

You will need a workspace that will accommodate all your equipment. For the digitization of photographs, you will need:

- A work area for a computer and a scanner for capturing and editing your photos
- An area to hold all your physical books
- An area to set up your camera, tripod, lights, and book cradle, if you are choosing to digitize your rare books and manuscripts with a digital camera instead of a scanner

Digital Storage Space

Use the Digital Images by Size and Space Table to get an idea of how much space each page of your digitized book will need. This table is based on the Federal Agencies Digital Guidelines Initiative (FADGI) recommended minimum capture of 300 ppi. In the first column of the table choose the dimensions that match your book. The second column will list the file size of one page. Multiply that file size by the amount of pages your book has. This will give you an estimate of how much storage space you will need per book.

Digitization Workflow

In-House Digitization

If you have decided to complete the digitization in-house, use the In-House Workflow Chart (figure 6.2) as a guideline for your project.

Prepare the Rare Books and Manuscripts

Step 1: Inspect for damage. Check the materials for signs of deterioration and/or damage.

Inspect for physical damage. Physical damage like rips or tears will need to be fixed by a conservator. Because of the high value of these materials, it is not recommended that you attempt to treat any damage yourself, unless you have the conservation skills to do so.

Figure 6.1. Photographing the pages of a manuscript. Pictured are the Rev. Najeeb Michaeel, Walid Mourad, and Catherine Yono. *Wayne Torborg/Hill Museum & Manuscript Library (HMML), Saint John's University.*

Inspect for chemical deterioration. The most common problems seen in rare books and manuscripts are foxing and red rot. The American Institute for Conservation (AIC) tells us that foxing is the result of both mold and metal contaminants in paper, and it can appear as brown, yellow, or red stains on the paper, often in spidery spots or blotches. Removing the marks of foxing should generally be left to a skilled book conservator. The AIC describes red rot as a process of leather deterioration most commonly observed in vegetable-tanned leathers. When the tannin reacts with sulfuric acid, red rot is the result. Leather objects affected by red rot will go through a variety of stages. Particularly susceptible to this reaction is vegetable-tanned leather made between 1850 and 1900.[5] Unfortunately red rot can't be reversed, but there is a recommended treatment. Speak to a conservator about treating your affected materials with a red rot cocktail, which can help to restore leather surfaces by penetrating the leather and adhering the leather fibers together.[6]

Table 6.1. Digital Images by Size and Space

5 x 7	3.2 MB
8 x 10	7.2 MB
8 x 12	8.6 MB
10 x 15	13.5 MB
11 x 14	13.9 MB
12 x 18	19.4 MB

Step 2: Clean the materials. The Canadian Conservation Institute has some guidelines on how to properly clean rare books and manuscripts and what to avoid.[7]

Do:

- Dust the binding with a dry, lint-free cloth, a soft-bristled brush, or a vacuum cleaner with cheesecloth over the hose (to prevent loose pieces of paper or leather from detaching and being sucked into the vacuum cleaner).
- For more ingrained dirt you can use a white vinyl eraser like Magic Rub on any stable cloth and paper bindings in good condition. Be sure to remove all eraser particles with a brush and/or vacuum cleaner.
- Leather bindings should be brushed or vacuumed only.
- As with any cleaning method, first conduct a small test on an unobtrusive area.

Do Not:

- Use moisture to remove stains. This could disturb, darken, or remove the surface or dyes from your materials.
- Clean rough calf or suede leather with a powdered eraser, because the residue is difficult to remove
- Leather bindings should not be treated with oils or else blackening will occur.

Prepare the Equipment: Scanner Method

Step 1: Clean the scanner. Clean your scanner by spraying glass cleaner on a lint-free towel and wiping the glass. If you have any glass parts that are prone to fingerprints, make sure that they are cleaned before each use.

Step 2: Regularly maintain the scanner. Clean the scanner on a weekly basis when in use.

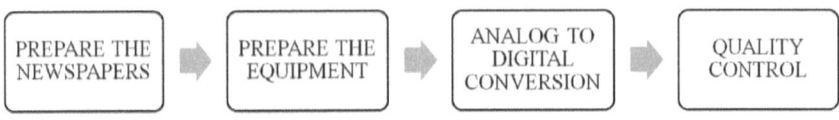

Figure 6.2. In-House Workflow Chart for Rare Books and Manuscripts

Prepare the Equipment: Digital Camera Method

Step 1: Place rare book or manuscript in a cradle.

Step 2: Set up the digital camera on a tripod.

Step 3: Set up two strobe lights with lighting umbrellas, positioned so that they even out the light source.

Step 4: Take photo, making sure that you have the desired focus, exposure, and composition.

The IFLA has some tips for preserving and recreating as much of the look and feel of the original object as possible:

- Capture bound volumes from cover to cover, including flyleaves, empty pages, pastedowns, the spine, and the page edges.
- Include a linear scale with the image in order to properly convey to the researcher the size of the original object.
- Scan pages one at a time.
- A sheet of paper or a piece of cardboard should be inserted behind damaged pages for extra support.
- Place a white background behind any translucent pages to avoid the image on the next page bleeding through.
- To accurately recreate the color of the original object, at least one page or image from the object should contain a color target to aid in color calibration.[8]

Analog to Digital Conversion

Using the guidelines from the Federal Agencies Digital Guidelines Initiative (FADGI), the master file format for your digital objects should be either TIFF, JPEG 2000, or PDF/A format. The recommended resolution should be set between 300 ppi and 400 ppi (300 being the lowest acceptable rate). The recommended bit depth should be between 8 and 16 (8 being the lowest acceptable rate). The recommended color space to use is either Adobe RGB (1998), ProPhoto, or eciRGB_v2. FADGI also recommends that these digital objects are in color.[9]

From your master file, you will create an access file. FADGI guidelines state that no image retouching of master files will be permitted. You may

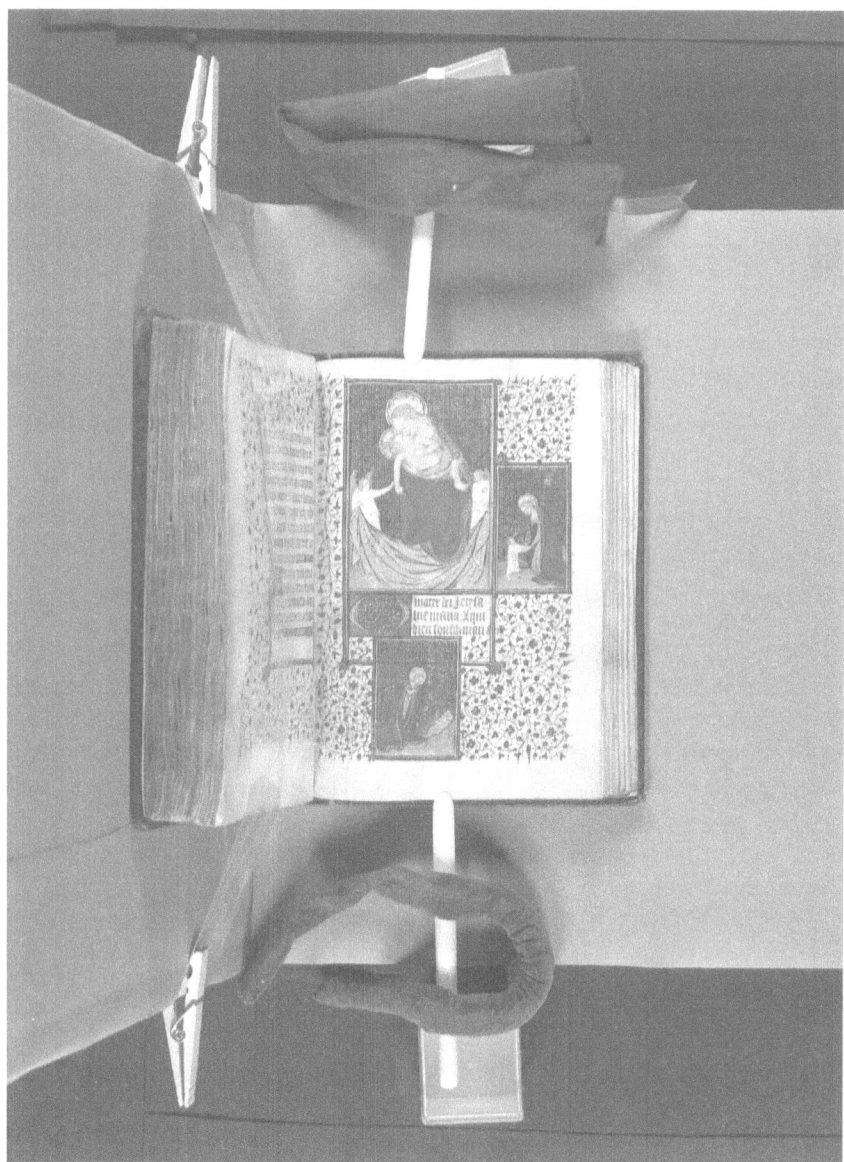

Figure 6.3. A medieval manuscript page positioned for photography. *Courtesy of Harvard Library, Imaging Services.*

wish to make a copy of your master TIFF, JPEG 2000, or PDF/A file, retouch that image, and then create a smaller JPEG file for access. Finally, you will save all of your files. Keep the original unedited files in a master files folder. Keep edited files and JPEG files in an access folder.

Quality Control

You must perform quality control and make sure that all digital objects are created according to best practices and your organization's standards; if you have not done this, you must attempt to digitize them again. If you are working with a large collection of items, it is acceptable to spot-check digital objects by a certain number of intervals for quality. For example, you can spot-check every tenth image for quality control. You must check your Optimal Character Recognition (OCR) text files as well. Also check that files are named correctly. *See* File Naming *section in this chapter for more information.*

Outsourcing Digitization

If you decide to outsource digitization, you will still need to have a workflow in place that staff can follow (see figure 6.4).

1. Document the rare books and manuscripts being outsourced. Make a list of all the materials that you are sending out for digitization.
2. Inspect the collection before sending. List the condition of each object.
3. Properly pack the materials. Create a set of instructions on how to properly pack your rare books and manuscripts and make sure staff

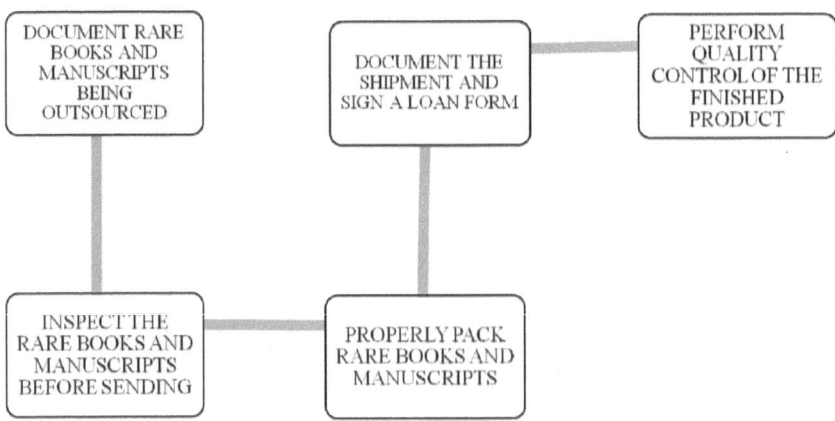

Figure 6.4. Outsourcing Digitization Workflow Chart for Rare Books and Manuscripts

follow the instructions. For their rare book digitization project, The Dumbarton Oaks Research Library used a custom-built crate, which contained archival quality boxes housing three or four books packed flat. Inside of those archival-quality boxes were three layers of preservation quality foam for each book. Each book was placed on its respective middle piece of foam and then traced out. After removing the book, a special knife was used to cut the foam, leaving a custom-made hole for the book to be placed in and perfectly protected.[10]
4. Document the shipment and sign a loan form. Somewhere in your project notes you should list the date that your books were shipped to the outside vendor, and you should make sure you have a copy of a signed loan form.
5. Perform quality control of the finished project. Check the digital files received and make sure they are to your satisfaction. Also make sure that you check the list you created in step 1, in order to confirm that all rare books and manuscripts sent out were returned and that they are still in the same condition as when they left your possession. You must take extra care with rare books and manuscripts, as they are prone to theft.

DESCRIBING THE COLLECTIONS

File Naming

There are various ways to name the digital files of rare books and manuscripts. For each book, you can choose to name the folder by the call number or another identifying number. You can name files inside this folder by the call number, followed by the sequence in which the image should be placed. So, the digital file of the front cover of a book would be JK154_1788_001. Alternatively, you can come up with some abbreviations for unnumbered pages, such as FC (front cover), BC (back cover), PDFC (Pastedown Front Cover), or PDBC (Pastedown Back Cover), and use numbers for numbered pages only. In this case the digital file of the front cover of a book would be JK154_1788_FC. Whatever terms you use, make sure they are consistent.

METADATA

Wendy Johnson, the copy cataloger for the Dumbarton Oaks Rare Book Digitization Project, emphasizes that "creating metadata for digitized books is to provide an experience of reading and paging through a digitized book as though it were a physical object. This involves describing every nuance of the organization of a book and its components from front cover to back cover, and includes the spine and edges."[11] The value of rare books and manuscripts is not only in their intellectual content but in such things as their binding, paper and illustration processes, so proper documentation of these elements through proper metadata is very important.[12]

The Library of Congress recommends capturing the following metadata:

- Title
- Creator
- Creation date or start date and end date
- Place of publication
- Publisher, producer, and/or distributor
- ISBN
- Other relevant identifiers (e.g., DOI, LCCN, etc.)
- Edition
- Subject descriptors
- Abstracts

PROVIDING ACCESS

Choosing a Platform

When choosing an access platform that will work for your digitized rare books and manuscripts, you'll want to make sure it has the following features:

- Search Capabilities: Users should be able to search available metadata, as well as the full text.
- Browsing Capabilities: Users should be able to search by subject, date, and/or author.
- Navigation: Users want to look at your digital objects in the same way they would look at the physical objects, so make certain that the access platform allows for page turning and image zooming.

Promotion and Marketing

Let's look at various ways organizations have promoted their digital rare book projects.

- Blogs: A blog can be a great way to promote your digital collection. WordPress and Blogger are the most common platforms used to create blogs. Blogs created by institutions to help promote their rare books include the Catholic University of America's blog *Ascendonica*, Princeton

University Library's blog *Notabilia*, and the University of North Carolina at Chapel Hill's blog *The Chapel Hill Rare Book Blog*.
- Instagram: This platform is primarily used for photos and videos. Users can like your posts and comment on them. Institutions that have utilized Instagram to promote their rare books and manuscripts include the Beinecke Rare Book & Manuscript Library at Yale University, the Rare Book Department of the Free Library of Philadelphia, and the Thomas Fisher Rare Book Library at the University of Toronto.
- Flickr: This platform is primarily used for images, which can be tagged for easy searching. Institutions that have utilized Flickr to promote their rare books and manuscripts include Northern Illinois University, the Lillian Goldman Law Library at Yale Law School, the Beinecke Rare Book & Manuscript Library at Yale University, and the Grolier Club.

PRESERVATION

Preserving Analog Items

Temperature and Relative Humidity

According to the National Park Service, the recommended temperature for storing rare books and manuscripts is between 60 and 70 degrees Fahrenheit. The recommended relative humidity is between 40 and 55 percent. Relative humidity levels below the recommended range leave the pages of rare books open to brittleness, while relative humidity levels above the recommended range can lead to mold growth and foxing of book pages.[13]

Storage

Rare books and manuscripts should be stored on metal shelving with a baked enamel finish. Ideally you will want to avoid any wood shelving, to prevent the migration of acids from the wood to the rare books and manuscripts, but if you must have wood shelving it should be sealed (oak should be avoided completely because it the most acidic wood). If your rare books or manuscripts are fragile, they should be stored in custom-made boxes. The boxes should be sized to the book and be made of acid-free materials. Make sure that your rare books and manuscripts are lined up straight on the shelves and place large volumes flat on the shelves, making sure that these large volumes are stacked no more than three volumes high. If you have books of various sizes, you should try to arrange these books by size, since tall volumes placed next to short volumes are known to warp and become deformed over time. So, for example, if you have twenty books on a shelf, fifteen of which are short and five of which are rather tall, simply remove the tall books from the shelf and place them on another shelf. For each book you have removed from the first shelf, use a book block (a sturdy book form that is made of archival materials) in its place. The book block should be labeled with the rare book's full citation, along with a note as to the new location of the book.[14]

Handling

The Canadian Conservation Institute provides the following guidelines on handling rare books and manuscripts:

- When removing a book from the shelf, hold the book firmly around the center of its spine and ease it from the shelf.
- Do not pull on the headcap (the leather covering at the head and tail of a book), because this will damage the spine.
- Use both hands for large or heavy volumes.
- If you are removing a volume that is beneath another, remove the top volume first.
- If materials are removed for processing, cleaning, or conservation treatment, transport them on a book cart or in a cardboard box.[15]

Preserving Digital Objects

You will have both image files and optical character recognition (OCR) text files to preserve for this project. Based on FADGI recommendations, your master image files should be saved in TIFF, JPEG 2000, or PDF/A format for digital preservation, and your access files will most likely be saved as JPEG files. It is recommended that your OCR files be in PDF/A, PDF, or RTF format. For further details on digital preservation, see the guidelines in the Preserving Digital Objects section in chapter 3.

CONCLUSION

In this chapter you learned how to create and curate digital rare books and manuscripts collections. Using the priority list, you should create a list of which rare books and manuscripts to digitize, and using either the in-house or outsourcing digitization workflow charts you can properly digitize those rare books and manuscripts. You have learned that rare books and manuscripts are subject to theft and the more valuable an item is, the more likely it should be digitized so the original can remain secure. In addition, you have learned what type of metadata to capture for your project and you have been given examples of ways to promote your project. Use the Digital Rare Books and Manuscripts Project Checklist (table 6.2) as a guide to help you through your project.

Table 6.2. Digital Rare Books and Manuscripts Project Checklist

Steps	Checklist	Notes
Choosing What to Digitize	Have you used the priority rubric to create a priority list of rare books and manuscripts to digitize?	
Preparation of Rare Books and Manuscripts	Are any conservation techniques needed for your rare books and manuscripts?	
Preparation of Equipment	Have you checked all of your hardware and software settings to prepare for the conversion?	
Analog to Digital Conversion	Are your digital objects created in accordance with listed guidelines? Preservation File Format: TIFF, JPEG 2000, PDF/A Resolution Rate: 300–400 ppi File Bit Depth: 8-16 Color Space: Adobe RGB (1998), ProPhoto, or eciRGB_v2 Color: It is recommended that your digital objects are in color.	
File Creation	Have you created a preservation file for each image?	
	Have you created an access file for each image?	
File Naming	Have you chosen a file-naming convention, and are you ensuring its consistency across all project files?	
Metadata	Have you created and checked the metadata for your preservation files?	
	Have you created and checked the metadata for your access files?	
Access	Have you chosen an access platform for your digital project?	
	Have you generated promotion and marketing ideas for your digital project?	
Preservation	Are physical objects properly preserved according to best practices?	

Steps	Checklist	Notes
	Have you performed a checksum for your preservation file folder?	
	Have you performed a checksum for your access file folder?	
Storage	Have you saved your preservation files to storage?	
	Have you saved your access files to storage?	

NOTES

1. Kimberly C. Kowal and Christophe Martyn, "Descriptive Metadata for Digitization of Maps in Books: A British Library Project," *Library Resources & Technical Services* 53, no. 2 (2009): 108–20.

2. Judy G. Russell, "Copyright and the Newspaper Article," *The Legal Genealogist*, March 19, 2012, http://www.legalgenealogist.com/2012/03/19/copyright-the-newspaper-article/.

3. "Federal Agency Digital Guidelines Initiative," http://www.digitizationguidelines.gov/.

4. "Digitisation Projects and Best Practice," IFLA, December 9, 2014. https://www.ifla.org/node/6777.

5. Eva Falls and Lucas Simonds, "Red Rot," AIC Wiki, last modified August 20, 2014, http://www.conservation-wiki.com/wiki/Red_rot.

6. Renée Wolcott, "An Illustrated Guide to Book Terminology," Conservation Center for Art and Historic Artifacts, http://www.ccaha.org/publications/resources-for-book-preservation.

7. "Basic Care of Books—Canadian Conservation Institute (CCI) Notes 11/7, CCI Note Series, Government of Canada, last modified September 12, 2017, https://www.canada.ca/en/conservation-institute/services/conservation-preservation-publications/canadian-conservation-institute-notes/basic-care-books.html.

8. "Digitisation Projects and Best Practice."

9. "Federal Agency Digital Guidelines Initiative."

10. Sarah Bogart, "Rare Book Digitization Project," Dumbarton Oaks. March 10, 2017. Accessed March 26, 2018. https://www.doaks.org/newsletter/rare-book-digitization-project.

11. Bogart, "Rare Book Digitization Project."

12. Bogart, "Rare Book Digitization Project."

13. "National Park Service," Conserve-o-gram: Archival and Manuscript Collections and Rare Books. https://www.nps.gov/museum/publications/conserveogram/cons_toc.html#collectionpreservation.

14. "National Park Service."

15. "Basic Care of Books," https://www.canada.ca/en/conservation-institute/services/conservation-preservation-publications/canadian-conservation-institute-notes/basic-care-books.html.

Chapter Seven

Art Collections

DIGITIZATION

Choosing What to Digitize

In this chapter we will discuss paintings and other two-dimensional works of art. Use the rubric in the priority list from chapter 2 to determine which works of art you should include in your digital collection. Here is a quick recap of the selection criteria:

Value

Does your work of art have historical and/or research value? Does your work of art have a high monetary value? Valuable works of art are frequently targeted for theft, so you may want to prioritize digitizing your most valuable objects so you can keep originals in a more secure location.

Demand

Is this work of art in high demand? Do researchers regularly request this item? Do visitors usually request to view this item? If the item is in high demand it should be high on your priority list. An object in high demand can drive a lot of web traffic to you if available in a digital format. Increased web traffic can bring more awareness to your digitized collection, your regular collections, and the institution itself.

Condition of Materials

Works showing advanced signs of deterioration should be at the top of your priority list, but only if you have the resources to get them treated by a conservator. If you are pressed for time, you may wish to prioritize materials that are in the best condition, since damaged works will slow down the digitization process.

Legal and Ethical Issues

In the United States, an artist's rights over his or her artwork do not expire until seventy years after death. If the work you wish to digitize is covered by copyright you will need to get permission from the copyright holder, or you will need to research whether digitizing this work is acceptable under fair use. See the Copyright and Intellectual Property Decisions Flowchart (figure 2.1) in chapter 2 for more information on this topic.

Availability

A great majority of artwork is unique, so if your organization has not made the object available, chances are it is not already available. If you are aware of multiple copies of a particular work, check with the owners of the copy or copies to see if they have digitized this work of art. Remember that even if they have, you may still want to digitize your work if you can bring something new to the table; your digital object may be of higher quality, or your digital file may have captured the work in color while the other copy is only in grayscale.

Choosing Equipment

Hardware

The Federal Agencies Digital Guidelines Initiative (FADGI) recommends that paintings and other two-dimensional works of art be digitized with either a planetary scanner or a digital camera.[1]

Software

You will need photo-editing software for this project. Adobe Photoshop is a popular software, and so is GIMP, an open-source, free software that will allow you to edit your image files.

Space Requirements

Physical Space

You will need a workspace that will accommodate all your equipment. For the digitization of your works of art, you will need the following:

- A work area for a computer and a scanner for capturing and editing your artwork
- An area to set up your camera, tripod, and lights, if you choose to digitize your works of art with a digital camera instead of a scanner
- An area to place the physical objects to be digitized

Digital Storage Space

The amount of digital storage space will be based on the size of your physical objects and the size of the entire collection. A project that will digitize a dozen or so works of art that are smaller than eleven by fourteen feet is going to require significantly less storage space than a projects that attempt to digitize thousands of works, many of which may be oversized.

Digitization Workflow

In-House Digitization

If you have decided to complete the digitization of your artwork in-house, use the In-House Workflow Chart (figure 7.1) as a guideline for your project.

Prepare the Work of Art

Step 1: Inspect for damage. Check the work for signs of deterioration and/or damage.

Inspect for physical damage. Physical damage like rips, tears, or a damaged frame should be treated by a conservator prior to digitization.

Inspect for chemical deterioration. If you spot possible mold on your works, they should ideally be serviced by a conservator before you attempt to digitize them.

Step 2: Clean the materials.

A conservator usually needs to be called in if a painting needs cleaning, as it is not recommended that a nonprofessional attempt to clean one.

Figure 7.1. In-House Workflow Chart for Art Collections.

Prepare the Equipment: Scanner Method

Step 1: Clean the Scanner. Spray glass cleaner onto a lint-free towel and wipe the scanner glass. If you have any glass parts that are prone to fingerprints, make sure that they are cleaned before each use.

Step 2: Regularly Maintain the Scanner. Clean the scanner on a weekly basis when in use.

Prepare the Equipment: Digital Camera Method

Step 1: Place rare work of art on an easel or table, or hang it on a wall with a neutral background.

Step 2: Set up the digital camera on a tripod.

Step 3: Set up two strobe lights with lighting umbrellas, positioned so that they even out the light source.

Step 4: Take photo, making sure that you have the desired focus, exposure, and composition.

Analog to Digital Conversion

For paintings and other two-dimensional works of art, the Federal Agencies Digital Guidelines Initiative (FADGI) recommends that the master files of your digital objects be in TIFF format; this format gets a 4 out of 4-star rating. JPEG 2000 is also an acceptable format, but it only scores 1 out of 4 stars. The recommended resolution is 3,000 to 12,000 pixels on long dimension aka length (3,000 being the lowest acceptable rate), or a minimum 600 ppi. The recommended bit depth is between 8 and 16 (8 being the lowest acceptable rate). The recommended color space to use is Adobe RGB (1998), ProPhoto, or eciRGB_v2. The sRGB color space is also acceptable but only scores 1 out of 4 stars. FADGI also gives a 4-star rating to objects in color and a 1–2 star rating to objects in grayscale.[2]

From your master file, you will create an access file. Do not retouch your master file in any way (FADGI guidelines state that no retouching of master files will be permitted). Ideally, you will retouch a copy of your master TIFF or JPEG 2000 file, and then create a smaller JPEG file for access. To finish, you will save all your files. Store the original unedited files in a master files folder and store edited files and JPEG files in an access folder.

Quality Control

Upon gathering all of your digital objects, you should check to make sure they meet the standards decided upon for this project. If manageable, you should go through each digital object to check for quality control. If you have a large collection of digital objects, it is permissible to check every Nth object (when you decide on the number, be sure to document it in your project workflow chart). Also check that files are named correctly. *See* File Naming *section in this chapter for more information.*

Outsourcing Digitization

Even if you decide to outsource the digitization of your works of art, you will still need to have a workflow in place for staff to follow (see figure 7.2).

1. Document the works being outsourced. Make a list of all the materials you are sending out for digitization.
2. Inspect the collection before sending. List the condition of each object.
3. Properly pack the works of art. Create a set of instructions on how to properly pack each type of material (paintings, prints, sculptures, etc).
4. Document the shipment and sign a loan form. Somewhere in your project notes you should list the date that your works of art were shipped to the outside vendor, and you should make sure you have a copy of a signed loan form.
5. Perform quality control of the finished project. Check the digital files received and make sure they are to your satisfaction. Also make sure that you check the list you created in step 1, so that you can confirm that all works of art sent out were returned and that they are still in the same condition they were in when they left your possession. You must take extra care with any well-known works of art as they can be a target for thieves.

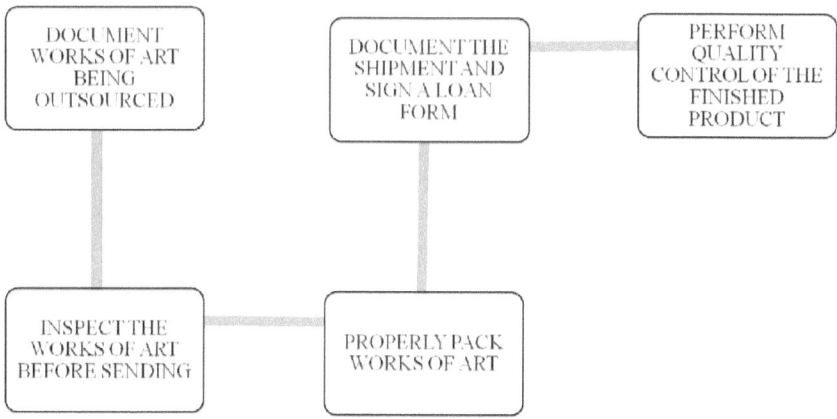

Figure 7.2. Outsourcing Digitization Workflow Chart for Art Collections

DESCRIBING THE COLLECTIONS

File Naming

If your works of art have accession numbers, you will want to include these numbers in the file name. If the artwork has a title, that may also be included in the file name. The artist's name may also be included in the file name. An example file name might look like this: 2008459_Lute Player_Valentin de Boulogne. The first part of the file name is the accession number, the second part is the title of the work, and the third is the artist's name. You do not want your file names to be too long, so you may consider using only the surname of an artist, rather than their full name or an abbreviated title, or you may forsake everything but the accession number for brevity.

Metadata

Institutions often have different requirements for metadata, so their choice of data standards are not always the same. When it comes to works of art and their visual surrogates, most institutions use VRA Core. The Library of Congress states that VRA Core is a data standard for the description of works of visual culture, as well as the images that document the works.[3] When deciding on a descriptive data standard, you will want to make sure that you choose one that allows you to capture the most common elements of a work of art, including the following:

- Catalog Number
- Copyright
- Creator
- Date
- Description
- Material
- Object Name
- Subject
- Title

PROVIDING ACCESS

Choosing a Platform

PastPerfect and CONTENTdm are popular with a lot of museums; however, if they are over your budget, some low-cost/no-cost open-source platforms that will work for your digitized art include the following:

- Omeka: a free, open-source tool with a focus on creating online exhibitions
- Collective Access: a free, open-source tool with a focus on cataloging and metadata
- CollectionSpace: a free, open-source tool for museums, libraries, historical societies, and other organizations with special collections

Promotion and Marketing

Getting the public involved in the digitization aspect of this project might be a good way to promote it. Think about putting a survey on your website asking people about which works of art in your collection they are interested in seeing digitized, and promote your survey on social media. Letting the public have input into what gets digitized may lead to a built-in audience once the project is completed and available.

Making your images downloadable is another way to promote your collection. If you allow the use of images for personal, educational, or noncommercial use, you encourage users to peruse your collections, giving them the opportunity to stumble upon a related collection they never knew existed and perhaps encouraging an in-person visit to your institution.

Finally, look for any opportunities to collaborate with another organization that may have a complementary digital collection. Think about putting together an online exhibit that is a blend of both of your collections. Collaborating offers the opportunity for a brand-new audience for both institutions.

PRESERVATION

Preserving Analog Items

Temperature and Relative Humidity

The temperature of both the gallery and the storage area should be between 68 and 72 degrees Fahrenheit. The relative humidity should be at 50 percent. Fluctuation in either temperature or humidity should be kept to a minimum.[4]

Storage

The National Park Service states that "framed paintings in stable condition can be stored safely and efficiently on storage screens."[5] You can purchase these screens or you can make them yourself, if you are so inclined. Paintings should be stored vertically, the only exception is for paintings that have loose or flaking paint; these works should be stored horizontally with the paint surface up.[6] You may use light cotton dustcovers over framed works of art or acid-free paper, but do not use plastic sheeting of any kind, as it may cause condensation.[7]

Handling

A framed painting should be carried with one hand at the bottom of the frame and one hand on the side of the frame. Unframed works should be held at the edges only, preferably while wearing thin, white, cotton gloves. Never handle more than one painting at a time, and use two people for large or oversized paintings.[8]

Preserving Digital Objects

Using the previously mention guidelines from FADGI, your preservation file should be a TIFF file, or a JPEG 2000 file if a TIFF file is not possible. You should keep multiple copies of your master file, in more than one place, and checksums should be completed regularly. For further details on digital preservation, see the guidelines in the section on Preserving Digital Objects in chapter 3.

CONCLUSION

In this chapter you learned the steps to digitizing, describing, and preserving works of art. We discussed how to describe the items in your new digital collection using VRA Core and how to provide access to your project with online platforms like Omeka, Collective Access, and Collection Space. Ideas to promote and market your project included surveying the public regarding what to digitize, making digital objects downloadable to increase interest in your digital collection, and possibly seeking out another institution for a collaborative online exhibit. Use the Digital Art Collection Project Checklist (table 7.1) to help you through your project.

Table 7.1. Digital Art Collection Project Checklist

Steps	Checklist	Notes
Choosing What to Digitize	Have you used the priority rubric to create a priority list of paintings/drawings/sculptures to digitize?	
Preparation of Works of Art	Are any conservation techniques needed for your works of art?	
Preparation of Equipment	Have you checked all of your hardware and software settings to prepare for the conversion?	

Steps	Checklist	Notes
Analog to Digital Conversion	Are your digital objects created in accordance with listed guidelines? Preservation File Format: TIFF, JPEG 2000, PDF/A Resolution Rate: 300–400 ppi File Bit Depth: 8–16 Color Space: Adobe RGB (1998), ProPhoto, or eciRGB_v2 Color: Color	
File Creation	Have you created a preservation file for each image?	
	Have you created an access file for each image?	
File Naming	Have you chosen a file-naming convention, and are you ensuring its consistency across all project files?	
Metadata	Have you created and checked the metadata for your preservation files?	
	Have you created and checked the metadata for your access files?	
Access	Have you chosen an access platform for your digital project?	
	Have you generated promotion and marketing ideas for your digital project?	
Preservation	Are physical objects properly preserved according to best practices?	
	Have you performed a checksum for your preservation file folder?	
	Have you performed a checksum for your access file folder?	
Storage	Have you saved your preservation files to storage?	
	Have you saved your access files to storage?	

NOTES

1. "Federal Agencies Digital Guidelines Initiative," accessed October 13, 2017, http://www.digitizationguidelines.gov/.
2. Ibid.
3. VRA Core Schemas and Documentation: VRA CORE - a data standard for the description of works of visual culture: Official Web Site (Library of Congress). Accessed October 3, 2017, http://www.loc.gov/standards/vracore/schemas.html.
4. Marjorie Shelley and Helmut Nickel, *The Care and Handling of Art Objects: Practices in the Metropolitan Museum of Art* (New York: Metropolitan Museum of Art, 2000).
5. "Conserve O Grams," Museum Management Program, National Park Service, accessed October 13, 2017, https://www.nps.gov/museum/publications/conserveogram/cons_toc.html.
6. Ross Harvey and Martha R. Mahard, *The Preservation Management Handbook: A 21st-Century Guide for Libraries, Archives, and Museums* (Lanham: Rowman & Littlefield, 2014).
7. Harvey and Mahard, *The Preservation Management Handbook*.
8. Shelley and Nickel, *The Care and Handling of Art Objects*.

Chapter Eight

Oral Histories

DIGITIZATION

Choosing What to Digitize

Use the rubric in the priority list from chapter 2 to determine which oral history recordings you should include in your digital collection. Here is a quick recap of the selection criteria:

Value

Does your oral history recording have great historical value to your community and/or researchers? The greater the historical value, the higher it should be on the priority list.

Demand

Is your oral history recording in high demand? Do researchers regularly request this item? If there is little to no demand, then place this item low on your priority list.

Legal and Ethical Issues

When working on your oral history project, you will want to make sure you protect yourself from any legal and ethical issues that may arise from your project. It would be foolish to spend a great deal of time and money on your project only to find yourself unable to use your oral histories because you did not protect yourself. First you will want to make sure you have permission to use the interview. The words spoken during an oral history interview are protected by copyright. This means that the interviewer and the interviewee will need to sign a release form, which will allow your institution to use the interview for publication, public programming, or other public dissemination.[1] Your institution may already have oral history release forms available, but older forms may not mention anything about availability through a website or the internet, so you will want to make sure that the release forms reflect current technology and future use. In addition, if you are not creating an oral history project from scratch but are instead converting analog oral histories into a digital format or making them digitally accessible, you may need to have new release forms signed by the interviewees to reflect that you want to make them available online. Your release forms should be customized to work for you and your organization, but make sure they include the following:

- Who has final ownership of the materials
- Transfer of copyright
- Expected uses of the materials
- Any restrictions on the materials
- A commitment to maintaining the highest professional and ethical standards for preserving and using the oral history interviews[2]

Both the interviewer and the interviewee should sign this form, in addition to the director of your oral history project. You should also consider having a consent form in addition to a release form. A consent form will include the following information:

- Interview Information. Approximately how long is the interview? What types of questions will be asked? Will the oral history be audiotaped, videotaped, or both?[3]
- Risks and Benefits. Make sure the interviewee is aware of both the risks and benefits of participating in this project.[4]
- Interviewee Rights. List the interviewee's rights. For example, if they are uncomfortable with any question, they don't have to answer it. If they want to drop out of the interview altogether they may do so. If they want to do the interview but prefer to remain anonymous, they may do so.
- Deposit of Materials. Here you will list where the materials produced during this interview will be stored. This includes the original files or audiotapes, videotapes, and transcripts, along with any copies.[5]

You will also want to protect yourself from libel law, which "provides redress for injuries to a person's reputation caused by statements that tend to expose a person to hatred, contempt or aversion, or to induce an evil or unsavory opinion of him in the minds of a substantial number in the community."[6] As an oral history interviewer, you are not exempt from libel laws because republishing libelous statements made by others makes you just as liable as if you made the statement yourself.[7] Indeed, when you make your oral history interview available, you the interviewer, the interviewee, and/or your institution can be sued by anyone who feels that a defamatory remark has been made about them within that interview.[8] As part of your oral history project you will need to make an effort to identify potentially defamatory statements made in interviews, and when you find a statement that could be damaging to a third party you should make certain that this portion of the interview is not made available to researchers or published.[9]

You will also need to be aware of ethical matters when it comes to oral histories. In order to have a successful oral history project it is important that there is a trusting relationship between the interviewer and interviewee. If at any point during the interview your interviewee wants to end the interview, you must respect their wishes and stop.[10] In addition, confidentiality must be respected. Everyone working on the project should sign a confidentiality agreement form. Your agreement form should include the following commitments:

- You will take all possible steps to protect the information received during the processing of (insert oral history name project here).[11]
- You will not disclose any personal identifying information to anyone (in person, via email, etc.) unless required under a court order.[12]

You should inform the interviewee of the measures that have been put in place to ensure their confidentiality.

Condition of Materials

Is the analog recording already showing signs of deterioration, or is it in fairly good condition? Recordings that are playable but showing signs of deterioration should be high on your priority list.

Availability

Is your oral history recording already available online? Chances are your oral history interviews are unique to your organization, but you should check if they are already online to avoid duplication.

Choosing Equipment

Hardware

Recommended hardware for digitization includes the following:

- Dual-tape cassette deck with noise reduction
- Large, over-ear headphones (preferable to in-ear headphones) with or without noise-canceling function
- A PC or Mac with at least 8 GB of memory
- PC sound card with support for 96 kHz/24-bit sampling

Software

You will need audio editing and recording software such as:

- Audacity
- AV Audio Editor
- WavePad
- Adobe Audition CC
- Sound Studio

Space Requirements

Physical Space

Digitizing analog recordings will require a workspace. Make sure you have the necessary physical space available before you begin. You will need:

- A work area for a computer, for capturing and editing your items
- An area to hold your cassette deck and headphones
- An area quiet enough to allow for audio editing

Digital Storage Space

Oral history interview files can take up a decent amount of space, so it is recommended that you have hard drive space of at least 500 GB. You may use your computer's internal hard drive or you may use an external hard drive for this project.

Digitization Workflow

In-House Digitization

If you have decided to complete the digitization in-house, use the In-House Workflow Chart (figure 8.1) as a guideline for your project.

Prepare the Analog Recording

Step 1: Inspect for damage. It is important to begin this process by visually inspecting the analog tapes, because they may reveal physical and chemical

Figure 8.1. In-House Workflow Chart for Oral History Collections

problems that will need to be dealt with to preserve them and to capture the best possible signals from them. You should not ignore any damage because physical and chemical problems may lead to serious damage during replay.[13]

Inspect for physical damage. Check the box and/or container for damage and breakage. If the container, reel, or cassette is damaged, the tape inside is also likely to have suffered damage or contamination. Check the interior of the container and the edges of the tape for indicators of the presence of mold. Tapes with mold can present a health hazard and should, therefore, be isolated and treated by professionals as soon as possible.

Inspect for chemical deterioration. Look for chemical deterioration of tapes containing a substrate of cellulose acetate (these were produced from the 1930s until the 1970s):

Typical deformations are caused by:[14]

- Different elongation and stretching properties of the components
- Hygroscopic tape components
- Vinegar syndrome
- Brittleness
- Deformation ("spoking," "cupping")
- Cracks

Look for chemical deterioration of modern tapes containing a binder of polyester-polyurethane (produced after the mid-1970s):[15]

- Pigment binder instability
- Decay caused by the hydrolysis process
- Sticky tape
- Oxide shedding

Step 2: Clean the tape. Analog magnetic tapes should only be cleaned when needed. Dirty or contaminated tapes may be cleaned of dust and debris with a soft brush and low-powered vacuum. Remember that mold can grow on tape after it has been exposed to high humidity (see figure 8.2). Tapes with mold should be isolated and treated by professionals as soon as possible because they can present a health hazard. If in doubt, consult an expert.

Figure 8.2. Mold on a Casette Tape. *Courtesy of Befog, Tapeheads.net.*

Order of cleaning:

- Vacuum cleaning, compressed air
- Careful mechanical cleaning (e.g., soft brushing, tissue wiping)
- Distilled water (if carrier composition allows)
- Chemical solutions (if carrier composition allows) [16]

Step 3: Tape restoration. To ensure the best possible transfer, the tape has to be in a smooth, playable condition. There is a risk that damaged spools can deform tape edges and affect the smooth transport of the tape. Damaged splices are a serious problem that are frequently encountered when working with analog tapes. For example, any gap between the tape ends exposes the adhesive, which will make the tape stick to the adjacent layer. In addition, the tape heads could be contaminated. If tape ends are overlapped or the splicing tape is too long, the tape may "thump" when being played.

Physical carrier restoration. Replace contaminated and/or broken spools. Repair bad splices. Add leader tape, if necessary. It is a good idea to replace old paper or plastic tape leaders with new, preferably acid-free paper leaders. Old adhesive must be removed using a solvent that does not damage the binder. Note that repairing splices and replacing leader tapes requires training by an experienced person because you may destroy something you cannot get back.

Chemical restoration. "Sticky" tapes suffering from pigment binder degradation can in most cases be brought into temporarily playable condition by special treatments like "baking," curing, or heated respooling. Such treatment should be undertaken very carefully and only if absolutely necessary.[17]

Step 4: Removal of print-through by rewinding. Print-through is the unintentional transfer of information from one layer to another layer of the tape reel. It reveals itself as echoes of the main signal. To minimize the print-through effect, wind the tape from end to end at least three times (but only if the condition of the tape allows it). Use reduced winding speed/tension during spooling on tapes that show signs of or that you suspect may suffer carrier degradation.[18]

Prepare the Equipment

Step 1: Use the latest playback machines. The availability of professional analog playback devices has dramatically decreased in recent years, as most of the manufacturers no longer produce analog machines or spare parts. A very limited range of new, professional tape machines is currently available. Professional machines have a greater ability to adjust replay parameters. They also have gentle tape-handling characteristics so that they do not damage the tape during replay. Also take into consideration the availability of spare parts! Use the most modern and professional replay machine possible. However, the machine must fully comply with format-specific parameters of the tape to be reproduced. Power up the machine before use to allow the electronics to stabilize.

Step 2: Clean the playback machine. The tape must be in very close contact with the heads in order to get good results. Dirt particles may easily cover the magnetic head gap, which causes additional loss in the playback signal.

Clean tape heads, tape guides, idlers, and capstan. Use isopropyl alcohol on a cotton swab. If there is anything that will not come off with this method, consult an expert. For rubber parts, do not use isopropyl alcohol, but plain water.

Step 3: Regularly maintain playback machines. The playback machine has to be regularly maintained to avoid quality loss in the transfer process and to prevent possible damage of the tape due to mechanical misalignment of the equipment. All transfer equipment has to operate within the specifications.

Analog to Digital Conversion

Step 1: File format. Accepted and standard preservation file formats include AIFF, BWF, and WAV. *See the section* Preserving Digital Objects *at the end of this chapter for more information.*

Step 2: Set a sampling rate. The International Association of Sound and Video Archives (IASA) recommends a minimum sampling rate of 48 kHz. However, for some types of material, especially for tapes that suffer from excessive noise, higher sampling rates, such as 96 kHz or even 192 kHz, may be useful. At the moment, 96 kHz is regarded as a widely accepted standard.[19]

Step 3: Set a bit depth. IASA recommends an encoding rate of at least 24 bits to capture all analog materials.[20]

Step 4: Monitor the transfer. If you want to achieve a good quality transfer, you need to monitor the analog to digital transfer. Put on your headphones and listen to the recording, then adjust items as needed.

Quality Control

Make certain that all digital recordings created are satisfactory; if they are not you must attempt to digitize them again. If you are working with a large collection of recordings it is acceptable to spot-check digital recordings by a certain number of intervals for quality. For example, you can spot-check every tenth recording for quality control. Also check that files are named correctly. *See* File Naming *section in this chapter for more information.*

Outsourcing Digitization

If your organization chooses to outsource digitization, you should follow the Outsourcing Digitization Workflow Chart (figure 8.3).

1. Document the recordings being outsourced. Make a list of all the recordings that you are sending out for digitization.
2. Inspect the recordings before sending. List the condition of each object.
3. Properly pack the recordings. Create a set of instructions on how to properly pack your recordings, and make sure staff follow the instructions.
4. Document the shipment and sign a loan form. Somewhere in your project notes you should list the date that your recordings were shipped to the outside vendor, and you should make sure you have a copy of a signed loan form.
5. Perform quality control of the finished project. Check the digital files received and make sure they are to your satisfaction. Also make sure

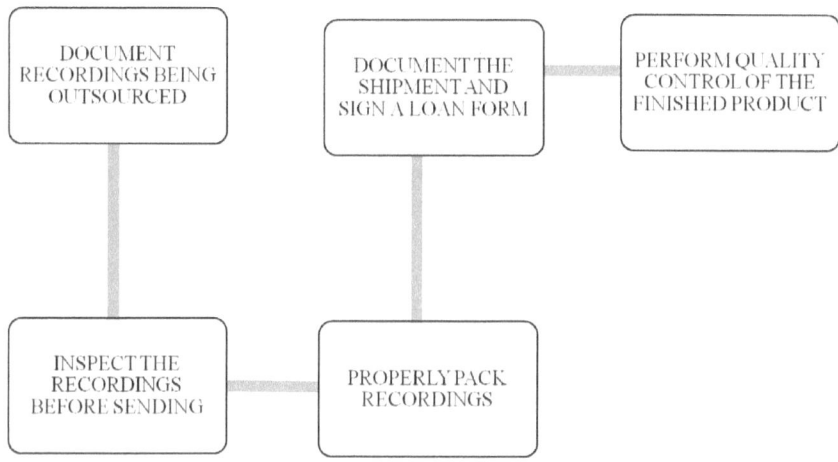

Figure 8.3. Outsourcing Digitization Workflow Chart for Oral History Collections

that you check the list you created in step 1, in order to confirm that all the recordings that were sent out were returned, and are still in the same condition as when they left your possession.

DESCRIBING THE COLLECTION

File Naming

When you create your digital file for each oral history interview, it is recommended that you name your files in the following format:

Interviewer, interviewee, the status, the part (represented in two digits), and the date (represented as YYYYMMDD). The options for status include:[21]

- Raw. The raw capture format
- Pres. The preservation copy
- Mez. The mezzanine copy, also known as the working copy or edit master
- Ed01. The edited version. The two-digit number at the end represents the version.
- Dis. The dissemination copy—the copy used for web access

The file should only use lowercase letters and be separated by underscores (for example: Anderson_Rodriguez_pres_01_20160801). Anderson is the interviewer. Rodriguez is the interviewee. The status is a preservation copy, thus "pres." This is the first part of the interview, thus "01" and the date of August 1, 2016.

All of these files will go into a directory with the project's name.

Metadata

Standards for audio metadata have been developed by a number of organizations, and include the following:

- The Audio Engineering Society. AES57-2011 is a standard that "provides a vocabulary to be used in describing structural and administrative metadata for digital and analog audio formats for the purpose of enabling audio preservation on those objects."[22] AES60-2011 is a standard that "addresses the creation, management and preservation of material that can be re-used as originally produced, or may provide input material for new production projects."[23]
- The International Association of Sound and Video Archives. IASA-TC02 details standards for ethics, principles, and preservation of audio material.[24]

There is no overall metadata system that has been developed specifically for oral history, but there are a variety of systems that are readily adaptable to the widely ranging needs of oral history collections, including Dublin Core, PBCore, MARC, MARC XML, MODS, and METS.[25]

You may find it useful to capture descriptive and technical metadata before, during, and immediately after the interview. Use the Oral History Metadata Table (table 8.1) to get an idea of what type of metadata it would be useful to capture.

PROVIDING ACCESS

Choosing a Platform

In this section we will look at some ideas for promoting and providing access to your oral history project.

The oral history project titled "Reservoir of Memories" is a collection of interviews from people with connections to the Mashapaug Pond/Reservoir Triangle area in Providence, Rhode Island.[26] In finding a way to present the project in a format that was accessible and preserved their work for the future, the project's team members chose to use Omeka.

They chose Omeka for two main reasons: (1) they had very little, if any, funding and Omeka offers a free option, and (2) the collection consisted of diverse formats, all of which Omeka could support. With any platform there

Table 8.1. Oral History Metadata Table

Interviewee and Interviewer Information	• Full name and any former name(s) • Address • Phone number • Email address • Birth date
Technical Information	• Length of the interview • Format of the interview • Audio settings • Video type • Video format • Amount of files and/or media types • Transfer medium • File names
Descriptive Information	• Short synopsis • Keywords • Proper names

Adapted from Louie B. Nunn Interview Information Form

are pros and cons to be aware of. The project's team members found that Omeka's appearance gave their project a very professional look, which they enjoyed very much. Another thing they liked about Omeka was the search feature, which made finding information easy. However, they found that the free version of Omeka lacked the necessary storage capacity for their project. To overcome this, highly edited interviews were put up as an alternative. They also did not like that Omeka offers no interactive component and that it lacks the capacity to facilitate online conversation.

Promotion and Marketing

One way to promote your oral history project may be through the creation of a podcast. A podcast opens the door to a wider audience and offers more exposure to your project. Additionally, creating a podcast is fairly simple and inexpensive. You may find that podcast inspires others to donate oral history interviews, or maybe they will be inspired to help with funding.

Equipment Needed

A podcast requires purchasing a small amount of hardware and software. You will need a computer with a reliable internet collection. The good news is that you may already have much of this already. In addition, you'll also need a small amount of staff. Take a look at the Podcast Requirements Table (table 8.2) for more information.

Once you have gathered all your resources you will want to create a workflow to help with the podcast process. Use the Podcast Creation Workflow Chart (figure 8.4) to help your organization create a podcast.

PRESERVING THE COLLECTION

Preserving Analog Objects

Ideally you will put your analog objects in long-term storage and will only need to retrieve them if a digital disaster should befall your organization and you need to start your digital archive from scratch. The following are guidelines for the long-term preservation of the oral history audiotapes you might have.

Environment

Keep your audio cassette collection in a cool, dry, dust-free environment. Store away from direct sunlight and fluorescent light. Do not store near combustibles like wood or cardboard. Avoid subjecting tapes to rapid temperature changes. Allow acclimatization before playing (four hours for every 18 degrees Fahrenheit change in temperature).

Storage

Fast-forward and rewind the tapes before storage. Make sure that the tapes are wound evenly and smoothly onto the cassettes. Store all tapes vertically in acid-free protective boxes or containers. Store in an area where the temperature stays lower than 70 degrees Fahrenheit. Avoid temperatures below freezing. Humidity should be between 20 and 40 percent RH (relative humidity). Do not store on wood shelving or in a basement or attic.

Handling

Make sure your hands are clean and free of oil, grease, and sweat before handling the tapes and that the area you are working in is free of dust. Do not

Table 8.2. Podcast Requirements

Computer	It should have a reliable internet collection.
Recording Equipment	To record the host's audio, you will need a digital recorder and an external microphone with a pop filter screen.
Staff	You will need a host, a producer, researchers, and writers.
Location	It should be quiet enough for the host to record their audio and achieve a consistent sound.

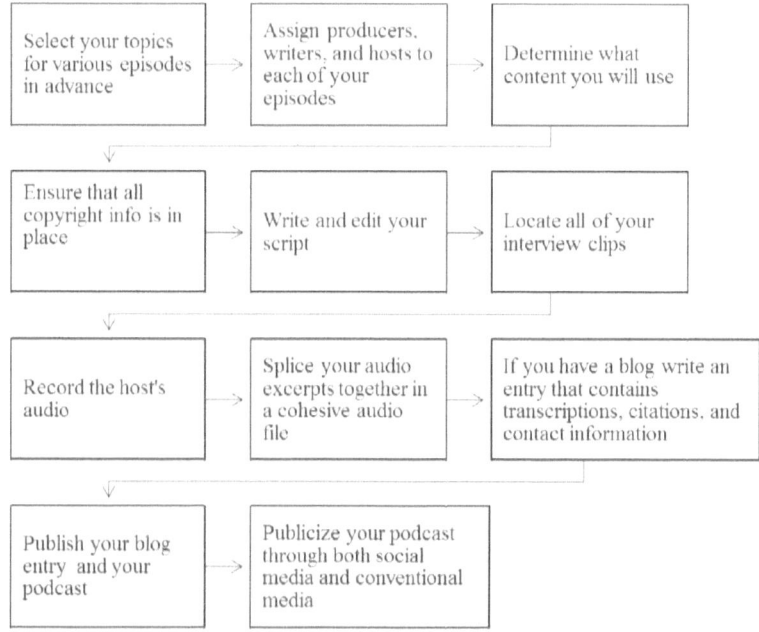

Figure 8.4. Podcast Creation Workflow Chart. *Adapted from the T. Harry Williams Center for Oral History Podcast Production Workflow.*

touch playing surfaces; handle the cassette tapes by their outer casings. Always wear gloves when handling original tapes.

Preserving Digital Objects

Your choice of file format should be one that ensures the long-term preservation of your digital objects. The two most widely used formats for digital preservation of audio materials are Broadcast Wave Format (BWF) and Wave Audio Format (WAV). Audio Interchange File Format (AIFF) is not as widely used but is also acceptable. The National Archives and Record Administration (NARA) does not recommend MP3 files because their use of lossy compression sacrifices quality.[27]

For further details on digital preservation, see the guidelines in the section on Preserving Digital Objects *in chapter 3*.

CONCLUSION

In this chapter you learned how to create and curate an oral history project. Using the priority list, you learned which items to digitize, and using either the In-House or Outsourcing Digitization Workflow Charts you can properly digitize your recordings. You are aware of the legal and ethical issues surrounding oral history interviews and recordings and you now know what type of metadata to capture for your project. You have also been given some examples of access platforms and promotion and marketing techniques from other organizations, and you have guidelines on the best practices for preserving your analog and digital objects. Finally, you have been provided with the Oral History Digital Project Checklist (table 8.3) to help you through your project.

Table 8.3. Oral History Digital Project Checklist

Steps	Checklist	Notes
Choosing What to Digitize	Have you used the priority rubric to create a priority list of recordings to digitize?	
Preparation of Recordings	Are any conservation techniques needed for your recordings?	
Preparation of Equipment	Have you checked all of your hardware and software settings to prepare for the conversion?	
Analog to Digital Conversion	Are your digital objects created in accordance with listed guidelines? Preservation File Format: AIFF, BWF, WAV Sampling Rate: 96 kHz File Bit Depth: 24	
File Creation	Have you created a preservation file for each recording?	
	Have you created an access file for each recording?	
File Naming	Have you chosen a file-naming convention, and are you ensuring its consistency across all project files?	
Metadata	Have you created and checked the metadata for your preservation files?	
	Have you created and checked the metadata for your access files?	

Steps	Checklist	Notes
Access	Have you chosen an access platform for your digital project?	
	Have you generated promotion and marketing ideas for your digital project?	
Preservation	Are physical objects properly preserved according to best practices?	
	Have you performed a checksum for your preservation file folder?	
	Have you performed a checksum for your access file folder?	
Storage	Have you saved your preservation files to storage?	
	Have you saved your access files to storage?	

NOTES

1. "3. Legal and Ethical Issues: First Things First," *Capturing the Living Past: An Oral History Primer*, Nebraska State Historical Society, accessed August 3, 2017, http://www.nebraskahistory.org/lib-arch/research/audiovis/oral_history/legal.htm.
2. Legal and Ethical Issues, Nebraska State Historical Society.
3. "University of Southern Maine," Informed Consent. Accessed March 26, 2018, https://usm.maine.edu/orio/informed-consent.
4. "University of Southern Maine."
5. "University of Southern Maine."
6. John A. Neuenschwander, "Oral History Interviews Lead to Libel Lawsuit," *OHA Newsletter* 34, no. 2 (Spring 2000), Http://www.oralhistory.org/wp-content/uploads/2008/10/opoha210.pdf.
7. Neuenschwander, "Interviews Lead to Libel Lawsuit."
8. "Libel and Defamation," accessed August 1, 2017, http://www.ohs.org.uk/ethics/libel.html.
9. "Libel and Defamation."
10. "Is Your Oral History Legal and Ethical?" Oral History Society, accessed August 1, 2017, http://www.ohs.org.uk/advice/ethical-and-legal/4/.
11. "Confidentiality Agreement Re. North Korean Film Project," accessed August 3, 2017, http://www.ohs.org.uk/ethics/confidentiality-agreement-NK.pdf.
12. "Confidentiality Agreement."
13. Mike Rivers and Graham Newton, "'Baking' Magnetic Tape to Overcome the 'Sticky-Shed' Syndrome," accessed March 6, 2017, http://audio-restoration.com/baking.php.
14. Rivers and Newton, "'Baking' Magnetic Tape."
15. Rivers and Newton, "'Baking' Magnetic Tape."
16. Rivers and Newton, "'Baking' Magnetic Tape."
17. Rivers and Newton, "'Baking' Magnetic Tape."
18. "Print-Through," A/V Artifact Atlas, accessed April 1, 2017, https://bavc.github.io/avaa/artifacts/print-through.
19. Iris Xie and Krystyna Matusiak, *Discover Digital Libraries: Theory and Practice* (Amsterdam: Elsevier, 2016).

20. Xie and Matusiak, *Discover Digital Libraries*.

21. Dean Rehberger and Brendan Coates, "File Naming in the Digital Age," in *Oral History in the Digital Age*, eds. Doug Boyd, Steve Cohen, Brad Rakerd, and Dean Rehberger. Washington, DC: Institute of Museum and Library Services, 2012), http://ohda.matrix.msu.edu/2012/08/file-naming-in-the-digital-age/.

22. Elinor A. Mazé, "Metadata: Best Practices for Oral History Access and Preservation," in Oral History in the Digital Age , eds. by Doug Boyd, Steve Cohen, Brad Rakerd, and Dean Rehberger (Washington, DC: Institute of Museum and Library Services, 2012), http://ohda.matrix.msu.edu/2012/06/metadata/.

23. Mazé, "Metadata," 2012.

24. Mazé, "Metadata," 2012.

25. Mazé, "Metadata," 2012.

26. Reservoir of Memories, https://reservoirofmemories.omeka.net/.

27. Edward M. Corrado and Heather Moulaison Sandy, *Digital Preservation for Libraries, Archives, and Museums* (Lanham: Rowman & Littlefield, 2014).

Bibliography

American Museum of Natural History. "Temperature and Relative Humidity (RH)." Accessed April 4, 2017. https://www.amnh.org/our-research/natural-science-collections-conservation/general-conservation/preventive-conservation/temperature-and-relative-humidity-rh/.

Association for Library Collections & Technical Services (ALCTS). "Definitions of Digital Preservation." Preservation and Reformatting Section, Working Group on Defining Digital Preservation. February 14, 2012. http://www.ala.org/alcts/resources/preserv/defdigpres0408.

A/V Artifact Atlas. "Print-Through." Accessed April 1, 2017. https://bavc.github.io/avaa/artifacts/print-through.

Baca, Murtha, ed. *Introduction to Metadata*. 3rd ed. Los Angeles: Getty Research Institute, 2016.

Beagrie, N. "Digital Curation for Science, Digital Libraries, and Individuals." International Journal of Digital Curation 1, no. 1 (2006): 3–16.

Billings, Victoria. "The Japanese-American Digitization Project: Collaboration to Tell a Story." CSU Libraries Network. January 20, 2015. http://libraries.calstate.edu/japanese-american-digitization-project/.

Boddie, Stefan. "What is METS/ALTO?" Veridian. July 19, 2014. https://www.veridiansoftware.com/knowledge-base/metsalto/.

Brown, Adrian. "Digital Preservation Guidance Note 1: Selecting File Formats for Long-Term Preservation." The National Archives. August 2008. https://www.nationalarchives.gov.uk/documents/selecting-file-formats.pdf.

"Confidentiality Agreement Re. North Korean Film Project." Accessed August 3, 2017. http://www.ohs.org.uk/ethics/confidentiality-agreement-NK.pdf.

Connecticut State Library. "Specifications for Digitizing the Newspapers of Connecticut." Accessed October 4, 2017. https://ctstatelibrary.org/newspaper_specs.

Cornell University Library. "Digital Preservation Management: Implementing Short-Term Strategies for Long-Term Problems." Accessed July 1, 2017. http://www.dpworkshop.org/dpm-eng/oldmedia/threats.html.

Corrado, Edward M., and Heather Moulaison Sandy. *Digital Preservation for Libraries, Archives, and Museums*. Lanham: Rowman & Littlefield, 2014.

Digital Humanities at Berkeley. "Choosing a Platform for Your Project Website." Accessed October 3, 2017. http://digitalhumanities.berkeley.edu/blog/13/12/04/choosing-platform-your-project-website.

Digital Memories. "JPEG vs TIFF for Scanning Photos, Slides, and Negatives." Accessed September 24, 2017. http://www.digitalmemoriesonline.net/scan/output/jpeg_vs_tiff.htm.

Falls, Eva, and Lucas Simonds. "Red Rot." AIC Wiki. Updated August 20, 2014. http://www.conservation-wiki.com/wiki/Red_rot.

Federal Agencies Digital Guidelines Initiative (FADGI). "Federal Agencies Digital Guidelines Initiative." Accessed May 25, 2017. http://www.digitizationguidelines.gov/.

Gertz, Janet. "Should You? May You? Can You? Factors in Selecting Rare Books and Special Collections for Digitization." *Computers in Libraries*. March 1, 2013.

Government of Canada. "Basic Care of Books—Canadian Conservation Institute (CCI) Notes 11/7. CCI Note Series. Updated September 12, 2017. https://www.canada.ca/en/conservation-institute/services/conservation-preservation-publications/canadian-conservation-institute-notes/basic-care-books.html.

Harvey, Ross, and Martha R. Mahard. *The Preservation Management Handbook: A 21st-Century Guide for Libraries, Archives, and Museums*. Lanham: Rowman & Littlefield, 2014.

Higgins, Sarah. "What Are Metadata Standards." Digital Curation Centre. February 2007. http://www.dcc.ac.uk/resources/briefing-papers/standards-watch-papers/what-are-metadata-standards.

Howard, Jennifer. "Storm Damage at NYU Library Offers Lessons for Disaster Planning in the Stacks." *Chronicle of Higher Education*. (November 23, 2012): A18–A19. http://www.chronicle.com/article/Storm-Damage-at-NYU-Library/135746.

InterPARES 2 Project: Terminology Database. InterPARES 2 Project. Accessed January 13, 2017. http://www.interpares.org/ip2/ip2_terminology_db.cfm.

Koelling, Jill Marie. *Digital Imaging: A Practical Approach*. Lanham: Rowman & Littlefield, 2004.

Kowal, Kimberly C. and Christophe Martyn. "Descriptive Metadata for Digitization of Maps in Books: A British Library Project." *Library Resources & Technical Services* 53, no. 2 (2009): 108–20.

Lefurgy, Bill. "Digitization Is Different Than Digital Preservation: Help Prevent Digital Orphans!" *The Signal* (blog). Library of Congress. July 16, 2011. https://blogs.loc.gov/thesignal/2011/07/digitization-is-different-than-digital-preservation-help-prevent-digital-orphans/.

"Libel and Defamation." Accessed August 1, 2017. http://www.ohs.org.uk/ethics/libel.html.

Library of Congress. "ALTO: Technical Metadata for Layout and Text Objects." Standards. Accessed October 3, 2017. http://www.loc.gov/standards/alto/.

Library of Congress. "Collections Care." Accessed May 15, 2017. https://www.loc.gov/preservation/care/scan.html.

Library of Congress. "Preservation Measures for Newspapers." http://www.loc.gov/preservation/care/newspap.html.

Library of Congress. "USNP Preservation Microfilming Guidelines." Newspaper and Current Periodical Reading Room, Serial and Government Publications Division. Accessed October 4, 2017. http://www.loc.gov/rr/news/usnp/usnpprepp.html.

Mazé, Elinor A. "Metadata: Best Practices for Oral History Access and Preservation." In *Oral History in the Digital Age*, edited by Doug Boyd, Steve Cohen, Brad Rakerd, and Dean Rehberger. Washington, DC: Institute of Museum and Library Services, 2012. http://ohda.matrix.msu.edu/2012/06/metadata/.

Monroe County Library System. "Digitization of Local History Material." Rochester Public Library - Central Library. Accessed January 9, 2017. http://www3.libraryweb.org/central.aspx?id=228.

National Digital Stewardship Alliance, Digital Library Federation. "Glossary." Accessed April 7, 2017. http://ndsa.org/glossary/.

Nebraska State Historical Society. "3. Legal and Ethical Issues: First Things First. *Capturing the Living Past: An Oral History Primer*. Accessed August 3, 2017. http://www.nebraskahistory.org/lib-arch/research/audiovis/oral_history/legal.htm.

Neuenschwander, John A. "Oral History Interviews Lead to Libel Suit." *OHA* Newsletter 34, no. 2 (Spring 2000): 1, 4–5. http://www.oralhistory.org/wp-content/uploads/2008/10/opoha210.pdf.

NISO Framework Working Group with support from the Institute of Museum and Library Services. *A Framework of Guidance for Building Good Digital Collections 3rd Edition*.

National Information Standards Organization. December 2007. Accessed June 20, 2017. http://framework.niso.org/.
National Information Standards Organization (NISO). "Collections Principle 4." Updated April 17, 2008. http://framework.niso.org/12.html.
National Information Standards Organization (NISO). "Collections Principle 9." Updated September 3, 2008. http://framework.niso.org/17.html.
National Information Standards Organization (NISO). "Metadata." http://framework.niso.org/24.html.
National Information Standards Organization (NISO). "NISO Publishes 'Understanding Metadata' Primer." Accessed April 20, 2017. http://www.niso.org/news/pr/view?item_key=163cc4576827006ed5adf7ef3b359416c4d94e15.
National Information Standards Organization (NISO). "Objects Principle 1." Updated September 3, 2008. http://framework.niso.org/37.html.
National Information Standards Organization (NISO). "Objects Principle 3." Updated April 17, 2008. http://framework.niso.org/20.html.
National Information Standards Organization (NISO). "Objects Principle 5." Updated April 17, 2008. http://framework.niso.org/22.html.
National Information Standards Organization (NISO). "Objects Principle 6." Updated April 17, 2008. http://framework.niso.org/23.html.
National Park Service. "Conserve O Grams." Museum Management Program. Accessed October 13, 2017. https://www.nps.gov/museum/publications/conserveogram/cons_toc.html.
Ogden, Sherelyn. "2.1 Temperature, Relative Humidity, Light, and Air Quality: Basic Guidelines for Preservation." Northeast Document Conservation Center. Accessed April 7, 2017. https://www.nedcc.org/free-resources/preservation-leaflets/2.-the-environment/2.1-temperature,-relative-humidity,-light,-and-air-quality-basic-guidelines-for-preservation.
Oral History Society. "Is Your Oral History Legal and Ethical?" Accessed August 3, 2017. http://www.ohs.org.uk/advice/ethical-and-legal/7/.
Peterson, Kit A. "What to Look for in a Scanner: Tip Sheet for Digitizing Pictorial Materials in Cultural Institutions. Washington DC: Library of Congress, June 2005. https://www.loc.gov/rr/print/tp/LookForAScanner.pdf.
Rehberger, Dean, and Brendan Coates. "File Naming in the Digital Age." In *Oral History in the Digital Age*, edited by Doug Boyd, Steve Cohen, Brad Rakerd, and Dean Rehberger. Washington, DC: Institute of Museum and Library Services, 2012. http://ohda.matrix.msu.edu/2012/08/file-naming-in-the-digital-age/.
Reservoir of Memories. https://reservoirofmemories.omeka.net/.
Rivers, Mike, and Graham Newton. "'Baking' Magnetic Tape to Overcome the 'Sticky-Shed' Syndrome." Accessed March 6, 2017. http://audio-restoration.com/baking.php.
Russell, Judy G. "Copyright and the Newspaper Article." *The Legal Genealogist*. March 19, 2012. http://www.legalgenealogist.com/2012/03/19/copyright-the-newspaper-article/.
Shelley, Marjorie, and Helmut Nickel. *The Care and Handling of Art Objects: Practices in the Metropolitan Museum of Art*. New York: Metropolitan Museum of Art, 2000.
Society of Rocky Mountain Archivists. "How to Flatten Folded Or Rolled Paper Documents." Accessed October 4, 2017. http://www.srmarchivists.org/resources/preservation/preservation-publications/how-to-flatten-folded-or-rolled-paper-documents/.
TownsWeb Archiving. "Optical Character Recognition (OCR) Scanning." Accessed October 4, 2017. https://www.townswebarchiving.com/ocr-scanning-service/.
"University of Southern Maine." Informed Consent. Accessed March 26, 2018, https://usm.maine.edu/orio/informed-consent.
University of Illinois at Urbana-Champaign. "4.0 Best Practices for Newspaper Preservation." University Library. Updated December 15, 2010. http://cms.library.illinois.edu/export/dcc/bestpractices/chapter_04_newspaperdigitization.html.
University of Illinois at Urbana-Champaign. "Newspaper Digitization." History Philosophy and Newspaper Library. Accessed October 4, 2017. https://www.library.illinois.edu/hpnl/about/digitization/.
Wolcott, Renée. "An Illustrated Guide to Book Terminology." Conservation Center for Art and Historic Artifacts. http://www.ccaha.org/publications/resources-for-book-preservation.

Xie, Iris, and Krystyna Matusiak. *Discover Digital Libraries: Theory and Practice*. Amsterdam: Elsevier, 2016.
Zarndt, Frederick, Brian Geiger, Robert Stauffer, Alyssa Pacy, Meredith Palmer, and Joanna DiPasquale. "Digital Collections: If you Build Them, Will They Visit?" Paper, IFLA WLIC, Singapore, 2013.

Index

access, 95; expanded, 4; providing digital collection, 40–41. *See also specific collections*
acclimatization, cassette tape, 110
ActivePaper Archive, 69
administrative metadata, 20
AIC. *See* American Institute for Conservation
ALTO. *See* Analyzed Layout and Text Object
American Institute for Conservation (AIC), 78
American Library Association, 5
analog preservation, 42–43
analog recording, for oral histories, 102–105
analog to digital conversion: art collection, 92; newspaper, 66; oral history, 106; photograph, 52; rare book, 80–82
Analyzed Layout and Text Object (ALTO), 69
application emulation, 15
art collections: access to, 94–95; analog to digital conversion, 92; choosing items to digitize, 89–90; describing, 94; digital project checklist, 96; digitization workflow, 91–94; equipment for digitizing, 90; file naming, 94; marketing and promotion, 95; metadata, 94; outsourcing, 93–94; preparing art work, 91–92; preservation of, 95–96;

quality control, 92–93; space requirements, 90–91
Audio Engineering Society, 108
audio recordings, preserving, 111. *See also* cassette tapes
authenticity, digital object, 35
availability, as selection criteria, 12, 13

backing up data, 17
bit depth, 106
bitstream preservation (bitstream copying), 17
books. *See* rare books
The British Library, 75
Broadcast Wave Format (BWF), 111
budget, 41, 44
Bulk Rename Utility (Windows), 39
BWF. *See* Broadcast Wave Format

California Digital Newspaper Collection, 70
California State University Japanese-American Digitization Project, 5
Cambridge Public Library, 69
cameras. *See* digital camera method
Canadian Conservation Institute, rare book cleaning guidelines of, 79
cassette tapes, 102–103, 105; cleaning, 103–104; mold on, 103, 104; removal of print-through by rewinding, 105; restoration of, 104–105; storage of, 110

checksums, 7
chemical deterioration, 78–79, 91, 103
chemical restoration, of cassette tapes, 105
CMS. *See* content management system
collaboration, digitization advantages for, 5
CollectionSpace, 55, 95
Collective Access, 95
color calibration, for rare books, 80
community, as access factor, 41
computer museum solution (hardware museum solution), 16
condition of materials, 12, 13; art collections and, 89; newspaper collection, 61–62; oral histories and, 101; photograph, 47; rare books and, 75
content creation, digital preservation goal of, 6
CONTENTdm, 55
content integrity, 7
content maintenance, 7
content management system (CMS), 7
conversion. *See* analog to digital conversion
copyright, intellectual property and, 19, 20, 62; decisions flowchart, 23

data archaeology (digital archaeology), 16
data backup, 17
deacidification spray, 71
demand, as selection criteria, 12, 13
descriptive metadata, 19
deselection, 18
digital archaeology (data archaeology), 16
Digital Art Collection Project Checklist, 96
digital camera method, 49, 80, 92
digital collections, 36; file naming guidelines, 37–39; marketing and promotion, 41, 55–56; metadata recording, 36–37; NISO principles for creating, 35; policy, 21, 23–25; providing access to, 40–41; reformatted and born, 6
digital curation, 8
digital curation projects: digital preservation policy for, 12–14; digital project checklist, 58; funding, 25–27; guidelines and principles, 14; overview, 11; selection criteria, 11–12; staff

responsibilities, 14. *See also specific projects*
digital life cycle, 8
digital preservation: challenges and threats, 18–19; choosing file formats, 43; considerations, 6; content creation goal of, 6; content integrity and, 7; content maintenance goal of, 7; copyright and intellectual property decisions, 19; cost factor and, 44; definitions, 5–6; digital curation and, 8; digitization differentiated from, 3, 7, 8; goal of, 6; metadata and, 44; multiple copy creation, 44; OASIS model for, 8, 14; physical security and, 44; policy, 12–14; security, 44; strategy, 14, 15–18; strategy criteria, 17. *See also* storage
digital project checklists: for art collections, 96; for newspapers, 72; for oral histories, 112; for photographs, 58; for rare books, 87
digital storage checklists, 32
digital storage space: art collection, 91; newspaper, 63; for oral histories, 102; for photographs, 51; rare books, 77
digitization: advantages of, 3–5; costs associated with, 5; creating good digital objects, 35; criteria, 11–12, 31; definition of, 3; digital curation and, 8; digital preservation differentiated from, 3, 7, 8; log, 32, 33; rubric, 13; space requirements, 32. *See also* analog to digital conversion; digital curation projects; equipment, digitization; hardware, digitization; outsourcing, digitization; *specific project type*
digitization workflow, 33, 34; art collection, 91–94; for newspapers, 63–67; oral histories, 102–106; for photographs, 51–54; for rare books, 77–82. *See also* outsourcing, digitization; *specific projects*
disaster management, 4–5
documentation, metadata, 19–20, 39–40. *See also* metadata; *specific materials*
Dublin Core, 39–40, 54, 108
Dumbarton Oaks Research Library, 82–83, 83

Index 121

Early American Fiction Collection, 76
Early English Books Online, 76
Early European Books, 76
Ehrman Medical Library, 4
Eighteenth Century Collections, 76
Electronic Records Archives Program, 17
elevator speech, 25–26
emergency recovery strategies, 16
emulation, 15, 16
English Books Online, Early, 76
equipment, digitization, 32
European Books, early, 76
expanded access, 4
Extensible Markup Language (XML), 36

FADGI. *See* Federal Agencies Digital Guidelines Initiative
Feature Set, 43
Federal Agencies Digital Guidelines Initiative (FADGI), 52, 71, 90, 92; on rare books, 80, 86
file formats, 43, 52, 72, 106
file naming, 37–38; bulk, 39; using numbers, 38. *See also specific collections*
film scanners, 62
fixity audits, 7
flash media, handling guidelines for, 22
flash storage, 19
foxing, 78
functionality, digital collection access and, 40
funding, 25, 26, 27; competition and, 26, 27; elevator speech, 25–26

gloves, 57

handling issues, 43, 57. *See also specific collections*
hardware, digitization: for art collections, 90; for newspapers, 62; for oral histories, 101–102; for photographs, 48–49; for rare books, 76
hardware museum solution, 16
headphones, 102
humidity, relative, 42
Hurricane Sandy, 4
hyperlinks, 37
hyphens, in file naming, 37

IASA. *See* International Association of Sound and Video Archives
IFLA. *See* International Federation of Library Associations and Institutions
in-house digitization workflow, 32, 33, 34; art collection, 91–93; newspaper collection, 63–66; oral histories, 102–106; for photograph collections, 51–52; for rare books, 77–82
insects, 42
intellectual property, 19, 20; decisions flowchart, 23
International Association of Sound and Video Archives (IASA), 106, 108
International Federation of Library Associations and Institutions (IFLA), 76, 80
interoperability, 43

Johnson, Wendy, 83

Langone Medical Center, 4
latex gloves, 57
legal and ethical issues, 12, 13; art collection, 90; libel law, 100–101; newspaper collections and, 62; oral history, 99–101; photographs and, 48; rare books and, 76
Library of Congress (LOC), 70, 71, 84, 94; ALTO and, 69; Prints & Photographs Online Catalog, 48
lighting, 50
LOC. *See* Library of Congress

magnetic formats, 19, 20
Making of America, 76
marketing and promotion: art collection, 95; digital collection, 41; newspaper collection, 69–70; oral history collections, 109; photograph collection, 55–56; rare book digitization and, 76–85
master files, 80; retouching, 52
media card reader, 50
medieval manuscripts, 76, 81
metadata, 8, 18, 43, 54–55, 68–69, 108, 109; administrative, 20; definition, 6; descriptive, 19; digital preservation and, 44; documentation, 19–20, 39–40;

preservation, 20; quality checks, 40; rare books and, 83–84; recording, 36–37; spreadsheets, 36, 54–55; standard selection for, 39
Metadata Encoding and Transmission Schema (METS), 69
Michaeel, Najeeb (Rev.), 78
Microsoft Excel, 36
migration, 15
mold, 42, 91, 103, 104
Mourad, Walid, 78
MP3 files, 111

National Archives and Records Administration (NARA), 17, 111
National Archives UK, 43
National Digital Stewardship Alliance, 7
National Information Standards Organization (NISO), 23–25, 35, 39
National Library of Australia, 71–72
National Park Service, 85, 95
NEDCC. *See* Northeast Documentation Conservation Center
newspapers: analog to digital conversion, 66; choosing digital objects, 61–62; digitization workflow, 63–67; equipment, 62–63; file naming, 68; handling, 71; marketing and promotion, 69–70; metadata, 68–69; OCR, 68–69; outsourcing, 66–67; preparing newspapers for, 63–64; preservation, 70–72; project checklist, 72; providing access to digital, 69–70; quality control, 66; repairing tears, 64–65; space requirements, 63; storage, 63, 71; unfolding and flattening, 65
New York University, 4
NISO. *See* National Information Standards Organization
nitrile gloves, 57
Northeast Documentation Conservation Center (NEDCC), 70, 71
numbers, in file names, 38

OASIS. *See* Open Archival Information System
OCR. *See* optical character recognition
Olive Software, ActivePaper Archive and, 69

Omeka, 55, 95, 108
Open Archival Information System (OASIS) reference model, 8, 14
open standards, file formats and, 43
operating systems emulation, 15
optical character recognition (OCR), 68–69
optical formats, handling guidelines for, 21
oral histories: analog to digital conversion of, 106; collection description, 107–108; digital project checklists, 112; digitization workflow, 102–106; equipment, 101–102, 109–110; file naming, 107–108; marketing and promotion, 109; metadata, 108, 109; outsourcing digitization of, 106; playback machine preparation, 105; preservation of, 110–111; providing access to, 108–110; quality control, 106; selection criteria, 99–101; space requirements, 102; storage, 102, 110
outsourcing, digitization, 33–34. *See also specific collections*

Pastedown Back Cover, 83
PAT. *See* Photographic Activity Test
PDF, file conversion to RTF or, 72
Photographic Activity Test (PAT), 56
photographs, 47; access to, 55–56; analog to digital conversion, 52; choosing, 47–48; cleaning, 51; digital project checklist, 58; digitization workflow, 50–54; equipment for digitizing, 48–50; file naming and, 54; metadata, 54–55; outsourcing digitization of, 53–54; photographing, 49–50; preparing and inspecting, 51; preservation, 56–57; quality control, 52; restoring, 51; scanning, 49, 50; software for digitization, 50; space requirements, 50–51
physical carrier restoration, 104
planetary scanners, 76, 90
plastic enclosures, 56
platforms: art collection, 94–95; choosing digital newspaper, 69; choosing digital photo, 55; oral histories and selection of, 108; rare book digitization, 84
playback machines, 105. *See also* cassette tapes

podcasts, 109, 110, 111
policy: copyright and intellectual property, 19, 20, 23; digital preservation, 12–14; review, 14. *See also* digital collection
preservation: analog item, 42–43; cost and, 4; digital object, 43–45, 57; metadata, 20. *See also* digital preservation; *specific projects*
Preservation and Reformatting Section of the Association for Library Collections & Technical Services, 5
Prints & Photographs Online Catalog, Library of Congress, 48
print-through, removal of, 105
priority list, for digitization objects, 12, 13
promotion. *See* marketing and promotion
provinyl chloride, 56
public domain, 62

quality control: for art collection digitization, 92–93; metadata, 40; oral history digitization, 106; for rare book digitization, 82–83

Rare Book Room, 76
rare books, 79; analog to digital conversion, 80–82; books and manuscripts preparation, 77–79; choosing, 75–76; cleaning materials, 79; describing collections, 83; digital project checklist, 87; digitization workflow, 77–82; equipment, 80; equipment for digitizing, 76–77, 79; file naming and, 83; handling of, 86; hardware, 76; in-house digitization of, 77–82; inspecting, 77–79; marketing and promotion, 76–85; metadata, 83–84; outsourcing digitization of, 82–83; photographing book pages, 78; preservation of, 80, 85–86; providing access, 84–85; quality control, 82–83; rare and fragile books, 4; resources, 76; software for digitization of, 77; space requirements, 77; storage of, 85–86
relative humidity, analog item preservation and, 42; art collections, 95; newspapers and, 71; photographs, 56; rare books and, 85
release forms, 100

Renamer (Mac), 39
"Reservoir of Memories", 108
Rich Text Format (RTF), 71–72
Rochester Public Library, 4
RTF. *See* Rich Text Format

sampling rate, 106
scanners, 49, 50, 62; cleaning, 51, 79; planetary, 76, 90; for rare book digitization, 76
security, 44–45
selection criteria, for digitization, 11–12, 31; for art collections, 89–90; newspaper items, 61–62; for oral histories, 99–101; photographs, 47–48; priority list for, 12, 13; rare books, 75–76
Smithsonian Institution Archives, 72
software, for digitization: art collections and, 90; for newspapers, 63; OCR, 68–69; oral histories and, 102; for photographs, 50; for rare books, 77
space requirements, digitization, 32. *See also specific collections*
special characters, file naming and, 37
spray, deacidification, 71
spreadsheets, metadata, 36, 54–55
standard, choosing metadata, 39; NISO guidelines for, 39
storage, 18, 19, 20; analog item, 42, 56; digital newspaper, 63
strategy, digital preservation, 14, 15–18

takedown policy, 12, 21, 22
tapes, analog, 102; cleaning, 103–104; inspecting, 103; removal of print-through by rewinding, 105
technical metadata, 20
technology preservation, as digital preservation strategy, 16
temperature, 85; analog preservation and, 42; digital preservation and, 18
theft, 45
Thibodeau, Kenneth, 17–18
tripods, 50

ubiquity, file formats and, 43
Ulukau Hawaiian Electronic Library, 69
underscores, file naming and, 37

value, 12, 13; art collection, 89; newspaper, 61; oral histories and, 99; photographs and, 47; of rare books, 75
Vassar College Libraries, 69
Veridian, 69
viability, digital preservation and, 43
viruses, 45
VRA Core, 54, 94

Wave Audio format (WAV), 111
withdrawal policy, 21

XML. *See* Extensible Markup Language
XML schemas, ALTO, 69

Yono, Catherine, 78

About the Author

Carmen Cowick is the director of preservation services at Preserve This, where she provides training, support, and consulting services for libraries in the areas of preservation and collections care. She received a bachelor's degree in art history and a master's degree in library science, with a certificate in archives and preservation of cultural materials from CUNY Queens College in New York City. Ms. Cowick has had several articles published in peer-reviewed journals and has given presentations at both regional and national professional conferences on preservation-related topics.

www.ingramcontent.com/pod-product-compliance
Lightning Source LLC
Chambersburg PA
CBHW022015300426
44117CB00005B/207